THE FUTURE OF BELIEF
DEBATE

THE FUTURE
OF BELIEF
DEBATE

Edited by

Gregory Baum, O.S.A.

HERDER AND HERDER

1967
HERDER AND HERDER NEW YORK
232 Madison Avenue, New York 10016

For permission to reprint the copyrighted material in this volume, the following acknowledgements are gratefully made: to *The Catholic World* for the article by Gregory Baum, O.S.A.; to *The Christian Century* for the article by Harvey Cox; to *Continuum* for the articles by James F. Anderson and H. de Lavalette, S.J., and part of the article by R. C. Hinners; to *The Ecumenist* for the articles by Arthur Gibson and Joseph Owens; to *The National Catholic Reporter* for the article by Eugene Fontinell; to *New Blackfriars* for the article by Brian Wicker; to *New Scholasticism* for part of the article by R. C. Hinners; to *Our Sunday Visitor* for the article by Barnabas Ahern, C.P.; to *Philippine Studies* for the article by John W. M. Verhaar, S.J. (the present article appears in abridged form); to *The Tablet* for the article by Illtyd Trethowan, O.S.B.; to *Theological Studies* for the articles by Bernard J. F. Lonergan, S.J. and Jaroslav Pelikan; and to *Triumph* for the article by Frederick Wilhelmsen.

Contents

III.

Introduction

GREGORY BAUM, O.S.A.

THE FUTURE OF BELIEF is a book of extraordinary significance. The strong reactions of Catholics and many Protestants have demonstrated this fact. Though it deals with philosophical issues and is, therefore, difficult to read, ordinary Christians have shown keen interest in Dr. Dewart's book. Why? Because it touches upon an issue that is close to them: the reconceptualization of the Christian Gospel. Many Christians of our day desire to speak about the reality in which they believe in a language and in terms that are in continuity with the ordinary experiences of life.

The world of scholars has also shown great interest in *The Future of Belief*. The number of significant book reviews is high. Since Dr. Dewart does not treat all the questions raised by him nor elaborate all the themes central to his thesis, his book is in need of study and commentary. The reviews have brought out with greater clarity the thought of Dr. Dewart and have clarified the contours of an important controversy in the Christian Church.

The collection of reviews made available here is by no means complete. Several significant evaluations have had to be left out. The choice has been largely determined by the desire to include reactions to Dewart's book from various professional viewpoints, from biblical science, from theology and from various philosophical positions. An attempt was made to avoid repetition. While Dewart has chosen the Thomism of Maritain and Gilson as his

7

principal adversary, the most vocal and most consistent opposition to him has come, not from this quarter, but from philosophers who themselves had reacted against the Thomism of Maritain and Gilson, namely, from the followers of Maréchal's interpretation of Thomism. This so-called transcendental Thomism is represented in this collection by more than one review.

An attempt was also made to signify the ecumenical and international interest of *The Future of Belief*. Protestant authors have been included as well as scholars outside North America.

Since reviews in this collection were written over a period of several months, the difficulties raised in the earlier ones are often examined in those written later so that the total effect of *The Future of Belief Debate* is a conversation involving the Christian intellectual community. It clearly emerges that the issue raised by Dr. Dewart will not come to rest. It will eventually involve the entire Christian Church in conversation.

After some hesitation the book reviews in this volume have been divided into two sections, one containing those reviews whose main drift or tendency is negative and the other containing those whose principal evaluation is a positive one. Since the reviews are sometimes nuanced in their judgment it has not always been perfectly clear in which section they belong. I hope that the reviewers will forgive the editor if they find their reviews in a section to which they had no intention of belonging.

Centre of Ecumenical Studies
St. Michael's College, Toronto

THE FUTURE OF BELIEF
DEBATE

I.

1.

A Theological Bombshell

ILLTYD TRETHOWAN, O.S.B.

PROFESSOR LESLIE DEWART'S book has had a very considerable impact in America and will probably cause a good deal of discussion in England. The excitement seems to have been caused partly by Dewart's proposals for the "dehellenization" of Christian philosophy and theology, and partly by the results which he anticipates as likely to follow from this, in particular a swift and radical development of dogma which will bring it into line with "contemporary experience." At first one might be tempted to lay the book aside as just another example of erecting "contemporary experience" into a sort of absolute, or another instance of that lapsing into secular humanism which is going on among American Catholics. But this would be a mistake. Dewart is a sincere and serious religious thinker, and makes some important points, although the theory of knowledge which is at the base of the whole discussion is, I believe, unsound.

His criticisms of "Scholasticism" are really criticisms of what may be called "conventional Thomism." For example, he thinks that Catholics have been regularly advocating "spiritual hedonism" ("The doctrine of St. Thomas, in the last analysis, rests on the hellenic principle that man's perfection *is* happiness"—p. 32). It is, I think, a fair criticism that Thomists make illegitimate play with the word "happiness." What man seeks, if he is true to his nature, is God—and his self-fulfillment lies in this. This is no novel conclusion, as Dewart later admits, and it seems to be all that he really wants. Again, his criticism of a doctrine of potency according to which "the development of anything which develops is intelligible only insofar as it is predetermined by the potency of that form from which it develops" (p. 45 n.) is also, in my judgment, acceptable. But when we come to his main thesis, the need for "reconceptualization" of the Christian doctrine of God, difficulties begin.

The first is that the discovery of God is discussed in terms of "commitment" (p. 59). It is true that we have to commit ourselves to the search for him, and that the discovery is *also* a commitment. But we must surely maintain that it *is* a discovery, although of a unique kind, if we are to talk about it at all. Dewart writes: "We cannot believe in God once-for-all any more than we can exist once-for-all. Faith must always realize itself, and God must always remain unrealized" (p. 65). This would be all right if it meant only that our awareness of God must always grow on pain of atrophying or turning into some sort of idolatry. But it has further implications. It proves to mean that "Christian belief implies a certain *conditional* disbelief in God which is merely the obverse of concern for the truth of belief. A genuine and lived concern with truth means a hypothetical willingness to disbelieve should the truth require one to do so" (p. 73).

Now I may imagine a situation in which I am bound in conscience to disavow the belief which I now have. But this does not involve the consequence that the belief which I now have must be an uncertain one. I realise that I could gradually lose it by not taking a proper interest in it—perhaps I could manage to forget it, and if I then pretended that I still had it I should only make matters worse. But this has nothing to do with the fact that I have it now. Dewart rightly complains that the conventional

14

Thomist account of faith does not justify faith's certainty (p. 71). He does not seem to realise that it is being replaced in Catholic theology by another account in which faith is an *experience* of God in his Church.

This introduces us to the fundamental instance of "de-hellenization," Dewart's thesis about knowledge and consciousness, which I find very difficult to follow. This seems to be the main line of it. Both we and the brutes "know," that is, "intentionally appropriate another being by some form of objectification." But the peculiarity of man is that he does not just objectify himself in knowing: "what is typical of [man's consciousness] is that it produces this experience: *myself,* that is my *self's-being*" (p. 82). This is not knowing an object, for I do not know myself as "other." From this the conclusion is drawn that "the typical form of human development can only be an increase in consciousness" (p. 83). Consciousness can develop only "by the differentiation of the self from objects," but the point of it is the "presence of being to itself, which constitutes the self."

"It follows then, if truth is the relation of man's intellectual life to his world, and if that relation is not established in the act of a faculty of man, but in the very constitution of man's being . . . that truth cannot be a mental faculty's conformity to things . . . Truth is . . . the adequacy of our conscious existence" (pp. 92–93). Although "continued development of the self can actually occur only to the degree that the world is objectified, that is, conceptualised, systematised, organized, *lived with* and *made meaningful* for our consciousness," that does not mean that "truth depends upon an external reality's *fiat* to the effect that the mind must conform to its requirements regardless of what the mind may need by its nature for its own existence and being" (pp. 93–94). So "the understanding of man's psychic life in terms of consciousness suggests a conception of truth in which substantial transformation of a man's understanding of being

15

does not necessarily imply unfaithfulness to an earlier, less well-developed stage of understanding. On the contrary, the normal course of man's intellectual life would require that whatever truth he may acquire be continuously surpassed" (p. 95).

I have thought it necessary to quote at length so that the reader may judge the matter for himself. If "truth" does not mean the mind's conformity to what is not itself ("external reality"), then we seem to be faced with a sort of Hegelianism and the question of general skepticism. It is surely a mistake to say that such a conformity is not "what the mind needs for its own existence and being." For what it needs is God increasingly found in the world and the developing world found in relation to God (who does not develop). This is a "conformity," although not a static one. What Dewart seems to be saying is that the continuity of truth as it develops is a matter of the mind's own development in a sense which makes the *content* of its knowledge, *what* it actually knows at any given moment, lacking in any permanent truth-value. The implications of this for the development of dogma will be obvious enough. And one would be forced to mention the obvious: that Christianity carries with it the acceptance as *true* (in the ordinary sense—which Dewart calls, disapprovingly, the "traditional" sense) of certain historical facts.

His theory of development rests, he says, "on the distinction between the *experience* and the *conceptualization* of faith" (p. 111). This would be all right if "experience" were recognised as *valid*. But it would also require us to say, I think, that we have a non-conceptual knowledge of God. This I believe to be the case. But Dewart seems to rule it out when he tells us that "with the substitution of consciousness for assimilative knowledge the distinction between language and thought disappears" (p. 104) and that "there can be no distinction between 'inner experience' and 'outer expression'" (p. 108). There is much more to the same effect in the central chapters of the book. It is the failure to get

16

behind concepts, I believe, that is ultimately responsible for the present "crisis of faith." To put it briefly, I must be content to say that the reaction against "mysticism" is the radical error. Dewart, however, thinks that the negative language employed by the mystics indicates a "relative disbelief" (p. 123).

But perhaps after all he does not really mean what he has appeared to mean. In an interesting discussion of modernism he speaks of the redemption as "having been accomplished as a concrete and discrete historical event" (pp. 115–116 n.). God "comes in person to deliver his message and, moreover, his message is not other than himself" (p. 137—on p. 8 we were told "Christianity has a *mission,* not a *message*"). Towards the end of the book he speaks of the "positive aspect of this concept of God, namely, his presence," quoting with approval Marcel's words about a presence which "reveals me to myself" by making me "more fully myself than I should be if I were not exposed to its impact" (pp. 176–177). This Dewart calls "the only valid 'proof' for the 'existence' of God that I know of." In principle I agree, and I should call this metaphysics. Dewart means by metaphysics primarily the text-book essence-and-existence business and therefore says that "God is not a reality of primarily metaphysical significance. He is rather a reality of primarily ontic import" (p. 200). And at the end he suggests, promisingly, that we should "reserve a special place for *silence* in *discourse* about God" (p. 214).

So, insofar as the book helps us to purify our thought about God, it is valuable. Many further criticisms of it could be made and many good points noted (among them the rejection of the conventional dichotomy between "sensation" and "intellection" and of much conventional talk about Providence). Its scope is a good deal wider than I have been able to indicate here. It seems to me that it falls into disastrous confusions, but it should certainly be read. To say that it "could be epoch-making" (Harvey Cox) is fantastic.

2.

The Permanence of Tradition

BARNABAS AHERN, C.P.

THE CONTROVERSIAL NATURE of this study on Christian faith has made it one of the most popular religious books of the year and a provocative target for varying reactions. Harvey Cox and several reviewers have hailed it as an utterly radical book that could be epoch-making. Others like Armand Maurer suggest that its post-Christian perspective indicates it is not Christian at all. Most readers, however, will probably refrain from formulating a personal judgment since they are not sufficiently familiar with earlier and modern philosophies to measure the force of Professor Dewart's argument.

He has set himself the task of confronting as a Christian philosopher the world of today, with which he is thoroughly conversant. He knows both by experience and study that, in a real sense, the world has come of age. Man's stream of self-consciousness has so deepened that thinkers of our time believe he has power constantly to re-create himself and to master his destiny. Corresponding advances in science and technology have convinced them that man holds the keys to the world's development, to the mastery of all its secrets and, therefore, to the formation of history itself. Progressive flux and advancing change are seen as the most fundamental law of human life, woven into its very fiber. The spirit of the world today is alive with a sense of almighty human power which fills man with awareness of his own transcendence, i.e., his openness to yet further stages of self-sufficiency and fulfillment.

As a man Professor Dewart knows by experience that his fellows have surged forward on a crest of self-understanding and scientific insight to a commanding competence which enthrones them as masters of themselves and of the world. As an intellectual he has studied the reflection of this spirit in the literary contributions of the world's great thinkers, measuring with precision and sympathy the insights of Freud and Marx, Bonhoeffer and Bultmann, de Chardin and Blondel. Though not agreeing totally with the variant emergents of contemporary philosophy he gives full credit to the validity of many of its insights and accepts them wholeheartedly as ingredients of the present human situation with which Christian belief in God must cope if it is to be relevant.

Professor Dewart, therefore, has accepted the challenge sounded by a world which, keenly aware of its own self-sufficiency, no longer feels any need for the tutelage of God. He does not dispute the real goodness of man's advance; he recognizes the folly of trying to turn back the clock. If man has arrived at his present state of intellectual maturity, it is the task of Christian thinkers to deal with him as an adult. To fulfill this task is the avowed purpose of this book. Professor Dewart has tried to resolve the colossal problem of rendering theism, the Christian philosophy of belief in God, relevant to our age.

Examining the traditional form of Christian theism he finds it completely wanting in relevance; its infantile wrappings (cf. p. 51) mute whatever message it might have for the mature man of today. Dewart sees in the Greek metaphysics which heretofore dominated the formulation of Christian faith a major obstacle to the present relevance of all previous systems. The expression of Christian belief in the vocabulary and thought patterns of Greek philosophy, though it may have served a relevant purpose in the bygone ages when man "thought as a child," is now meaningless for a world come of age. The absolute and static categories of Greek metaphysics, its explanation of reality on the basis of neat distinctions between essence and existence, potency and act, substance and accident, seem totally unreal to modern man who sees all life as an evolving process and all reality as meaningful only through its dynamic presence in human and world development.

For the author of this book, therefore, the future of belief depends upon the rejection of Greek philosophy as our form of expression for theistic faith (this he calls "dehellenization") and the development of an entirely new form in consonance with the mature mind of man in our day. In the light of this conviction, Dewart proposes (in Chapters 3 and 5) a tentative and exploratory delineation of the form and elements which would characterize the philosophic presentation of Christian faith in the days to come.

It is the opinion of this reviewer that Professor Dewart has done a real service in urging upon Christian thinkers the need to form a theism truly relevant to our age. He has shown convincingly that, if we are to reach the men of today, we must use their language and take cognizance of the praiseworthy advances which they have made in every field of knowledge and endeavor. Even more, our own thoughts about God are bound to be greatly enriched if we take into account modern man's insights into himself and the world around him.

This enrichment of Christian theism through use of contemporary thought and language is a compelling necessity for the fulfillment of the Church's mission to the men of today. Should the Church continue to express its theism in the terms of a philosophy alien to the modern world it will speak only to itself—with a voice which rumbles inarticulately in a vacuum. The very dynamism of a message depends on its relevance.

In a very real sense Professor Dewart is a model for all those Catholic intellectuals who would face the challenge of our times. Moving competently in the area of modern philosophies he has gleaned those elements which recur most frequently and which, therefore, are most widely accepted by modern thinkers as constitutive of man's experience and of the world's progress.

These elements provide both the materials with which he works and the vocabulary with which he expresses his proposed form for future faith. The theism of the future which he sketches in chapter five is, therefore, alive with modern insights. Though a thinker of today may disagree with Dewart's prognosis, he will at least find himself at home among words and concepts which are thoroughly familiar to him because thoroughly relevant to the age in which he lives.

The ordinary Catholic, on the other hand, will be considerably shocked by what he finds here. (I cannot but admire the courage of a man like Dr. Dewart who, for the sake of truth, is ready to speak the truth as he sees it, even though he knows the brick-bats will fly!) The source of shock is not only the ice-cold bath of the unfamiliar but, even more, the radical changes of perspective which will strike many as doctrinal shifts blurring the very lineaments of faith.

No one could be more aware than Dr. Dewart himself that his book, especially its fifth chapter, will rouse doubts about the orthodoxy of his proposals. He has, therefore, emphasized that his reconstructed form of theism is not definitive; he stresses that the character of his remarks is "tentative and exploratory." In other words, with the humility of a real scholar, Professor Dewart invites criticism in order that the observations of others may help him and all Catholic intellectuals in their efforts to shape a philosophic presentation of Christian faith which will be at once valid in itself and relevant to the needs of our time.

The author's request for criticism of his proposals, implicit in his stress on their "tentative" character, provides opportunity to point out what are the seeming weaknesses of his book. In my judgment there are several areas which clamor for reconsideration if the approach to contemporary theism is to follow a straight course along the lines which Professor Dewart has indicated.

(1) To be truly relevant to our time Christian theism must take its point of departure not only from man's sense of competence and mastery (focal in Dewart's treatment) but also from his painful and ever-growing sense of failure and human insufficiency. The latter experience, growing out of war and the rumors of war, racial tension, personal confusion and neuroses, divorce, suicide and blighting moral evil, is even more keenly felt by most men than the scientist's confidence in the infallible effects of technology. The jeremiads of the Psalmist are just as poignant today as when they were first uttered. Nor do we have any assurance that these dirges will ever cease; for, after all, the burden of sin, original and personal (no matter how a modern theist may explain it) shall always lie heavily upon us. As it was in the beginning, is now and ever shall be, the human person of every age must cry out with St. Paul: "What a wretched man I am! Who will rescue me from this body doomed to death?" (Rom. 7:24).

As a modern man, therefore—and as a man of all seasons weighted down by the burden of sin—I find it very difficult to accept with sympathetic understanding Professor Dewart's affirmation that "humility is not the recognition of our inferiority and God's superiority" (p. 205). Truth itself, which Dewart following St. Teresa singles out as characteristic of humility (p. 205), forces every man (and especially poor, confused, sinful modern man) to recognize that something is radically deficient in himself. As for the Christian, this bitter realization will instinctively prompt him to do what his fathers have always done and what his children always will do, to fall upon his knees before God (even though Dewart would absolve him from this—p. 204).

In other words, because the author of this book has not taken sufficiently into account man's enduring sense of weakness and failure, his whole discussion of "The Basis of Man's Religious Relations with God" (pp. 200–206) seems somewhat unreal to me, a Christian, even as it must seem unreal to all non-Christians who experience the *Angst* of existentialism. Whether believer or unbeliever, a reader of this section will hardly recognize himself in the "man" of whom Dewart speaks.

(2) To be truly relevant to our time a philosophic presentation of Christian faith must take into account not only process and progress, not only change and flux (so frequently highlighted by Dewart), but also the univocal constants of humanness, its solidarity in character and its unity in experience. Cultural changes have revolutionized the world and thrust it forward a long way since the time of William Shakespeare. A man of his day would hardly feel at home in the present world. Yet everyone of us can identify ourselves with the characters whom Shakespeare portrays, for in heart and flesh they were man like ourselves. In joy and sorrow, in laughter and tears, in marrying and begetting children, in personal thought and in reaction to other men, they are bound to us with an identity which none can mistake.

This static element in human experience, this univocal constancy in human nature, receives little attention in this book. Yet it is as much part of the human situation as the flux and change which Dewart emphasizes. If the latter element figures so largely in his philosophic formulation of Christian faith, why not also the former? The very reality of human nature itself as something monolithic in its durability, as something which remains always the same no matter what change or progress may come, —this, too, must be taken into account when one attempts to integrate Christian faith into modern experience.

If the concept of God is to be fitted into a pattern of change, it must also be fitted into a pattern of permanence. Man who changes remains always man; and, let us face the fact, in the depths of his humanness he is never altered by change. Abraham and Sara laughed and I laugh; Ezechiel cried and I cry; Paul suffered and I suffer; and each of us, in his gloaming years, returns to the weakness and tears and laughter of his childhood, for these things have always been with us. There is something rock-like in man which the winds of change do not alter and the waters of time do not melt away.

I wonder if this fact about man should not illumine our understanding of the development of Christian dogma (cf. Chapter 3) and serve as a directive element in our philosophic presentation of what Dewart calls the "reality" of God (pp. 173–185), His personality (pp. 185–189), His omnipotence (pp. 189–194), and His Eternity (pp. 194–200). If in human nature there is a character which never changes, if even in each individual man there is a depth of personal identity which remains untouched by time and change, what, then, must we say of Him who is the "rock" of His people?

(3) In the light of this last observation, I would ask Professor Dewart to rethink his strictures on previous forms of Christian theism. The Scholastic presentation of faith has its weaknesses. Perhaps its static and absolute conceptualizations do not make sufficient provision for the dynamism of all reality. But to say, as Professor Dewart does, that our previous theism is totally "child-

25

ish and infantile" (p. 51) like the relatively childish and infantile stage of evolution from which it comes sounds offensively cavalier. How much, for instance, the author's treatment of "The Personality of God" (pp. 185–189) would have gained if only he had read the Cappadocians and Didymus the Blind. Time and again he has deprecated the Scholastic principle of analogy; yet, in his treatment of "The Being and Existence of God" (pp. 173–185), he has simply translated this principle into modern terminology.

An author who would wipe out our previous theism with a clean sweep has overlooked the fundamental fact that the men who formulated it were, at heart, men like ourselves—certainly as intelligent as our modern intellectuals and just as devotedly Christian. It is true, they had no idea of the remarkable progress which would come after their day; but they did know human nature which never changes. To make light of the wisdom of the past and to discount it completely in ministering to the present world is to assume the attitude of an "angry young man" who is completely at odds with the past because he does not really know the present. No intellectual, therefore, can afford to be an "angry young man," if he would remain truly intellectual.

Could it not be that the static forms of Scholastic theism, which Dewart decries, have sublimely represeted the mystery of living permanence in God as it is mirrored in the living permanence of man, his unchanging personal identity? "I" and "Thou" are essential to all dialogue, whether between man and man or man and God. But unless the "I" and "Thou" retain that static sameness which we call identity, dialogue becomes only a meaningless fracas of empty voices. For the true dialogue of Christian faith both God and man must remain "the same—yesterday, today, yes, and forever." To me, therefore, the absolute and static character of Scholastic formulation serves to emphasize an element in our theism which is as relevant to modern man as the dynamic character of a formulation, like Dewart's, based on change; for modern man (like the men of all ages) is both changing and changeless. A theism of the future will be both unreal and irrelevant unless in some way it conserves the spirit which breathes through the "absolute" and "static" formulations of the past.

(4) There is a last area which I suggest as a constant control and a life-giving source for every future philosophic formulation of Christian faith. This is the area of fidelity to the New Testament. Faith, if it is truly Christian, must be a share in the human response of Christ the man to the self-manifestation of God. This response He has described for us in words which are now treasured in the Gospels and unfolded in the epistles. It is true, as Professor Dewart points out, the integration of theism with everyday experience requires the "demythologization of Scripture" (p. 49). But, as every student of Scripture knows, there is a limit to demythologization.

When a sacred writer expresses his mind with the thought-patterns, imagery and vocabulary of his own cultural background, his ideas can become meaningful for men of a different age only when they are reinterpreted in a contemporary cultural form. But there is no need for demythologization when, as happened time and again, Christ and the writers of the New Testament used words which belong to humanness itself and which, therefore, endure through all human change, in every culture and at all times. Such words are a transparent medium through which the mind of Christ becomes manifest to us. They become, therefore, the rule of Christian faith, since He is at once "the Mediator and the fullness of all revelation" (Vatican II, *Dei Verbum,* 2).

Certainly the philosophic presentation of the truths which He uttered will have little similarity to the words He used— "Father-Son," "life-death," "bread-water-light," "love-hate"—

but, at the same time, they must be ruled by the words He used. Otherwise we shall not minister to men of our day a real philosophy of Christian faith. For it is the very nature of philosophy that it should correspond with reality; and the only reality we can present, when we present Christian faith, is the mind of Christ.

Because Professor Dewart presents in his fifth chapter what he considers a tentative Christian theism of the future, I think it would be well if he were to check everything he has written there to see if it truly and fully accords with the revelation of God as it is presented to us in Sacred Scripture.

It would be unwarranted to conclude that these observations are deprecatory of the purpose, spirit, or methodology of this book. I esteem Professor Dewart for the competence and courage which he has shown in undertaking a task which is essential for the real dynamism of the Church's mission. It is my sincere hope that he will continue and perfect the labor which he has here begun. Whatever, therefore, I have written is intended only as a suggestion which might bring greater solidity and relevance to his work.

3.

The Past of Belief:

Reflections of a Historian of Doctrine

JAROSLAV PELIKAN

ALTHOUGH LESLIE DEWART'S *The Future of Belief* is an essay about the future addressed by a philosopher to theologians, it embodies certain judgments about the past which seem to call for reaction from a historian of Christian doctrine. For while "the retelling of the whole history of Christian dogma from the apostolic age until our own day" (p. 132) is not its purpose, it does purport to be based on "the conclusion[s] of historical research." At least three of these conclusions seem to require comment.

THE HELLENIZATION OF CHRISTIANITY

Professor Dewart explicitly dissociates his interpretation of "hellenism" from that of Harnack (p. 133), on the ground that Harnack thought of the process of hellenization as a corruption, while Dewart thinks of it as a stage of development once useful but no longer relevant. Thus he calls for "dehellenization of dogma, and specifically that of the Christian doctrine of God" as

29

his program (p. 49). What is the specific content of this hellenism? It seems to include such notions as "the hellenic principle that man's perfection *is* happiness" (p. 32), "the hellenic philosophical viewpoint" which equates "intelligibility and necessity" (p. 44, n. 38), "a hellenic idea that development must be reducible to becoming" (p. 44), "the presumed Truth of God's self-identity, which is a hellenization of the Christian experience" (p. 74). This "hellenization of Christian philosophical speculation . . . [constitutes], in point of historical fact, the condition of the possibility of modern atheism" (p. 153). Applied to the doctrine of God, hellenism brought it about that God was "fittingly conceived as a suprarational person" (p. 187), and it was in this way responsible for the doctrine of the Trinity. Summarizing his interpretation of this history, Dewart states (p. 136):

But it would be unhistorical to suppose that at the first moment of the development of the Christian consciousness this consciousness could have created the concepts whereby to elaborate itself—it is not until our own day that such a possibility has begun to emerge. At the time, all it could possibly have done was to use the concepts of which it was *already* possessed. The intellectual effort of the early centuries was, therefore, predominantly directed to the adaptation of hellenic conceptions to serve the development of dogma—that is, to the casting of Christianity in hellenic forms.

Even apart from the condescending tone of this paragraph (of which more a little later), it seems to rest on a partial and distorted reading of "the intellectual effort of the early centuries." It is instructive, for example, to study the development of Christian doctrine in a cultural and intellectual ambience that was decidedly non-hellenic—the Syriac. The description of the relation between Jesus and God in the theological tractates (or "homilies") of Aphrahat—which can be studied even by some-

30

one who does not read Syriac, thanks to the translation of Fr.
Parisot and the monograph of Fr. Urbina—shows a Christology
that is quite orthodox according to the standards of fourth-
century Christian "hellenism," but that is not obliged to resort to
the technical terminology which Dewart finds to be so dated.
And *pace* Dewart's disclaimers, the language of Aphrahat, even
in its unabashedly "mythological" cast, speaks with a directness
to which the present-day reader may sometimes resonate more
readily than he does to "hellenic" language. But that assumes
that the language of orthodox dogma is in fact hellenic. Thus
Dewart presents his version of the history of the Christian notion
of *logos* (pp. 139–41) without referring either to its absence
from the Nicene Creed (whose use of the name "light" for God
has, he claims, "lost its meaningfulness . . . completely" [p.
214]) or to its relations with the *chokhmah* of Proverbs 8. As
the history not only of *logos* but of all the major terms (including and especially *phōs ek phōtos,* as I have argued elsewhere)
demonstrates, the Trinitarian and Christological dogmas were as
much a fundamental refutation of hellenism as they were some
sort of "adaptation of hellenic concepts." Failure to observe the
nuances of his history leads the author to the amazing historical
postulate of a "hellenism in which *natura, substantia* and *persona*
were realities of common experience" (p. 146). Such a refusal
to take history seriously is "hellenic" if anything is.

THE DEVELOPMENT OF DOGMA

A large part of *The Future of Belief* is given over to an examination of the problem of doctrinal development. Dewart suggests
"that loyalty to the Catholic Church would be best safeguarded
. . . by a theory of development that would integrate contemporary experience and faith" (p. 90), a theory that would "account

not only for the possibility of *ontogenetic* but also *phylogenetic* development" (p. 97). He believes that both the discovery of organic evolution and the contemporary understanding of the nature of consciousness make possible a theory of the development of dogma in which authentic change and novelty can be acknowledged, and he sees this possibility as a uniquely modern discovery. "Of course," he writes, "the idea that . . . orthodoxy *requires* the development of dogma, has not occurred to the Christian mind until recent times" (p. 150).

Just what Dewart means by "recent times" in this context becomes explicit in a historical judgment that occurs at least twice in the course of his argument. He claims to be able to discern historically "Christianity's conscious decision, especially since the end of the eighteenth century, to avoid developing dogma as far as possible" (p. 108). Somewhat later he expands this thesis and speaks of "a policy which Christianity unconsciously began to develop at some time between the days of patristic hellenism and the age of medieval Scholasticism, and which had been implicitly espoused since the beginning of the sixteenth century and consciously abided by since the end of the eighteenth" (p. 172). It would seem, then, that there has been a development not only of dogma but also of resistance to the idea of development: from the unconscious to the implicit to the conscious. Elsewhere we are told of "a partly conscious, partly unconscious, commitment to a supposedly final conceptualization" (p. 135). There is an intriguing analogy between this theory about the development of hostility to development and the very theory about development of dogma which Dewart excoriates. To a historian of doctrine who is not a Roman Catholic, moreover, there is some irony in the designation of the end of the eighteenth century as the point when Christianity (= Roman Catholicism) consciously decided to avoid developing dogma; for 1854, 1870, and 1950 are the specific points at which the development of dogma was not only acknowledged *de facto* but promulgated *de jure.* It is significant in this connection that Marian doctrine, which has become the *cause célèbre* of the problem of development of dogma, especially since *Munificentissimus Deus,* is mentioned, as far as I can tell, only once in the entire book, and then in a brief footnote (p. 199, n. 25). The earlier *cause célèbre* of development of dogma, which played a role in relations with the East somewhat similar to that played by Mariology in relations with Protestantism, was the Double Procession; this, too, is disposed of in a footnote: "And, to be sure, *filioque*" (p. 142, n. 18). But since these developments of dogma helped to precipitate schism between churches rather than between the churches and "a world come of age," they appear to be irrelevant to the central thesis.

For underlying the historical judgments about development of dogma appears to be an even more basic historical judgment: "It is not until our own day that such a possibility [for Christian consciousness to create the concepts whereby to elaborate itself] has begun to emerge" (p. 136). This helps to explain a parenthetical remark near the beginning of the book about "the contemporary world, which is the only real one" (p. 16). The charges of "undevelopment" and the calls for further development are based on the assumption that past developments represented an accommodation to their times, such that *"natura, substantia* and *persona* were realities of common experience" in "hellenism" (p. 146), and on the assumption that the adult world of the twentieth century demands a development of dogma that will catch up with its maturity. But if the underlying problem is an understanding of Christian doctrine that has absolutized the past, or, in the language of Dewart's article in *America* (Dec. 17, 1966), "loved the past too long," is it really much of an improvement to absolutize the present moment instead? For as there are aspects of revelation which Christians today find *simpático* and others from which they feel alienated, so previous ages in the history of the Church have had to struggle to come to terms with the whole of Christian truth, boggling at some of the very things which have assumed such importance for believers today. The development of Christian doctrine has not been a unilinear progress, but has been characterized by an openness simultaneously to the past and to the present, while heresy has attempted either to absolutize a particular stage in the development (so Semi-Arianism in relation to Nicaea) or to sacrifice continuity to relevance (so Modernism).

THE CRISIS OF CONTINUITY

Near the end of his book Dewart refers to the "crisis of authority" (p. 204), suggesting that it "may be at bottom the crisis of absolute theism"; and he contemplates rather dispassionately "the eventual disappearance of Christianity in the form in which we have known it since primitive times." Thus it would seem that the deeper crisis is a crisis of continuity; for if "the form" (singular, with definite article) of Christianity "since primitive times" is to disappear, all previous discontinuities—between the apocalyptic and the institutional, between *geistliche Vollmacht* and *kirchliches Amt,* between Jewish and non-Jewish observance, *et illud omne genus*—seem together to constitute "the form." The author does refer to "the faithful continuity of the truth of [Christian] doctrine" (p. 109). He is sure that "continuity in truth requires the continuity of God's self-communication to man, and the continuity of man's correlative religious experience in response to God's initiative" (p. 114).

Yet when the book gets down to specifying what it means by continuity, the picture becomes rather different. The cool acceptance of discontinuity in Church dogma is matched by the as-

sumption that "Judaeo-Christianity is in uninterrupted temporal
and cultural continuity with the history of man" (p. 123);
likewise, authentic faith takes place in "the continuity of achiev-
ing-belief and achieved-belief" (p. 65). Therefore, Tillich's
reference to "the classical theology of all centuries" is repeated
several times (pp. 38, 39, 40, 48) in a polemic against his failure
to be as radical in his reinterpretation of the doctrine of God as
he was in his use of the doctrines of the Trinity and the Incarnation. The historical assumption behind such discussions as these
seems simultaneously to exaggerate and to minimize the continuity in the history of Christian doctrine: to exaggerate it, because
despite an oblique reference to Theodore of Mopsuestia (p.
150), it ignores the variations within patristic doctrine or, for
that matter, within medieval doctrine as represented by the Vic-
torines, Scotus, or Cusanus; to minimize it, because despite the
reiteration of the word "belief," it is with concepts and theories,
not with beliefs and practices, that the author is chiefly concerned. Worship is referred to occasionally, as in the suggestion
"that the Christian theism of the future might so conceive God as
to find it possible to look back with amusement on the day when
it was thought particularly appropriate that the believer should
bend his knee in order to worship God" (p. 204). As nearly as I
can tell, there is no explicit reference to prayer. Yet certainly one
defensible definition of "Christian theism" would be: an attempt
to give an account in concepts of the belief at work in the
Christian practice of prayer. The practice of prayer has undoubtedly fluctuated in the history of the Church, as it does in the
history of every Christian. But in the light of Professor Dewart's
rejection of "the distinction between language and thought" (p.
104), is there not some massive continuity in the daily repetition
of the Our Father "since primitive times"? To coin a phrase,
securus judicat orbis terrarum. Again, is the continuity in the
celebration of the Eucharist, in the administration of baptism, in

the preaching, teaching, and reading of Scripture, in obedience to the gospel purely formal and external? Even on Dewart's own terms, it cannot be.

A colleague used to say that present-day seminarians "don't know just what it is they ought to have such difficulty believing." Precisely because I am, if anything, more radical than Dewart in my concern for "the future of belief" even though I am considerably less sanguine than he about "a world come of age," I wish that there were less oversimplification and caricature in his description of the past of belief. For I suspect he might find in that past some of the very resources he seeks. The questions might become more complex, but the answers more profound.

4.

Beyond Neo-Thomism

H. DE LAVALETTE, S.J.

ECLIPSING THE SIMPLE BOOKS on the secular mentality, or the death of God, at last we have in *The Future of Belief* a theological work which contends with fundamental problems. Reflecting philosophically upon the content of the Christian faith, the author shows himself to be far more faithful to St. Thomas than many neo-Thomist manuals of theology. Consequently, this book joins with other efforts attempted elsewhere (for example, J. B. Metz in *Christliche Anthropozentrik*), and adheres to the theological trend which, like Rousselot and Blondel, has definitely rejected any apologetical attempt for natural belief. Moreover, the book is timely because of its discussion which wishes to take seriously the tenets of Scholastic thought. In effect, we are witnessing a *chassé-croisé* between Catholics and Protestants. Catholics attempt to cope with contemporary thought and Protestants, especially the Germans to be sure, are becoming interested in St. Thomas. Serious in both subject and purpose, this book is often penetrating in its analyses and reveals a real gift for striking formulas. All the more reason, then, that it ought to be submitted to criticism.

St. Thomas is often considered merely as the representative of Scholastic thought. And the latter is the quintessence of a hellenization of the Christian faith which we will discuss later. Nevertheless, it seems regrettable that the author embraced, in one and the same criticism, St. Thomas and his degenerate successors. Why not take advantage of the accomplishment of recent research? Is it not to render the tasks a little too easy by criticizing a Thomism represented by authors who share in no way his own preoccupations? There is, on the other hand, the Thomism of Metz and Rahner (*Geist in Welt*), and the Thomism advocated by Hans Urs von Balthasar in *Herrlichkeit* 3/1.—a work which includes but surpasses by far the project of the author. It is Balthasar who, speaking about the distinction of essence and existence in St. Thomas, recalls this basic idea: *"Esse rei, quamvis sit aliud ab ejus essentia, non tamen intelligitur quod sit aliquod superadditum ad modum accidentis, sed quasi constituitur per principia essentiae"* (Met. 4, lect. 2, no. 558). A simple consideration by the author of the above principle, would have saved him the trouble of writing at great length in rejecting current erroneous interpretations.

The author's stand is negative. It is by the term "dehellenization" that he characterizes (negatively) that which he aspires to (positively) (cf. pp. 49–50). In other words, one ought not to give an exaggerated importance to the negative analyses of the author, who certainly reacts against his own neo-Scholastic training. The French reader can't help but recall Laberthonnière who, half a century ago, followed the same path to conclusions very close to those of the author. Moreover, their criticisms are often the same: for example, against the hedonism of Thomistic morality. Heidegger certainly brought this theme back into fashion. Catholic theologians are similarly preoccupied, and it would have been praiseworthy had the author put himself on the level of the actual discussion. (Cf. the articles "Eudémonisme" from *Dictionnaire de Spiritualité,* and on hellenization, by A. Grillmeier, in *Scholastik,* 1958.)

However, the problem is not to know if a hedonistic reading of St. Thomas is possible. We do not contest whether this could have been the case. Actually, there are several ways of reading ancient authors, be they pagan or Christian, Greek or Latin. We can never come to a reading of St. Thomas equivalent to that of one of his contemporaries (even if such is the task, asymptotically, of an historian of ideas). Not only on the level of non-scientific reading (and who can pride himself with a perfect scientific reading?) do we form anachronisms without end; and worse, the reading of certain modern commentators illustrates how we posit problems in St. Thomas which were not his own (the solicitude for a presence of God here and now and for a faith which is not uniquely oriented toward salvation in the future life, is a Catholicism which reacts against the preaching ensuing from the Restoration). This is not absolutely forbidden. It is even very fruitful, provided one knows what one is doing. In France, Aubenque gave us last year an "Existential" Aristotle!

The matter, in reality, is to give an interpretation to Thomist "hedonism" appropriate for our time, which takes into consideration not only the Marxist criticisms of middle-class success, but also those of Heidegger or of Sartre against the pretentious happiness of the inauthentic good conscience or of Freudian illusion. We do not want to cauterize Thomist "hedonism."

The author's aversion to metaphysics is far more positively a denunciation of the danger of confusing the faith with its representations. We have become, in effect, very sensitive to the difference between the faith and the manner in which the faith is conceptualized (representations of the faith). One ought always to take care when bringing back past representations to a lived faith, not to hypostatize them for themselves. Let us express this in medieval terms: *intellectus fidei* is a secondary movement in relation to *auditus fidei* and leads to a more profound *auditus fidei*. Faith does not exist in an adult without representations. Thus it is not a question of "comparing" an unnameable Reality and its various representations. But we ought to criticize representations spontaneously received, in other words, received from culture. Which, again in medieval terms, means to apply *ratio* to *auctoritas* (*auctoritas* being that which is received from culture—from the hellenized Fathers as well as Scripture!). Dogmatically speaking, theology is never identified with faith (faith is not gnostic), nor with a confession of faith (faith such as is "represented" in articles of faith).

The author, with good reason, places theology in the movement of faith toward God—a God who is never actually totally present to the totality of our life. It is true that this "relativity" of the faith, well recognized by the Augustinian belief in God, provides an insight for a doctrinal development on the level of collective history.

This relativity, however, does not make faith *conditional* as the author would think. The *credere in Deum* is linked to the *credere Deo*. It is impossible to believe in God without at the same time believing that faith originates in the revelation of God himself: no one comes to the Father except by me. Moreover, one cannot argue from a moral duty to follow conscience, which is never totally fixed. For credibility is never exterior to faith: *non crederet nisi videret esse credendum*. Faith has an appropriate certitude, very real although nonscientific.

The considerations of the author on faith appear much clearer if one relates them with the end of the book. It is with a profound reflection on God, a rejection of God as "Supreme Being" produced by metaphysics and by the representations of personality, Omnipotence and Eternity associated with him, that the author expects a renewal, or more exactly, a development of theology. By remaining with a metaphysical God, one remains with a God that is unbelievable, and even more, nondemonstrable. It entails being enclosed in ontological representa-

40

tions, in an all-too-human idea of God. To be sure, the author spends more time in denouncing than in showing.

However, one perceives where he wants to lead us. Fortunately, the way is not simply a negative theology. Nor is it only toward a God "for consciousness." The author shares much with modern philosophy: the meaning of consciousness, of human transcendence in relation to nature, which is surely above an affirmation of a demiurge, a God for men as revealed by faith who could not but be revealed in the faith (since God is not "a number" among beings, as St. Thomas again would say). This is where the author would lead us.

Having attained this level of consciousness where the Totally Other is present, it remains to be shown that God is not a projection but the Reality who has his own identity, his own nature—his glory, as von Balthasar would say. In his own manner, the author expresses what so many contemporary authors strive to articulate: only a very pure God, the God of the mystics is believed today. And it seems to me a perfectly good reason to see in our incapacity to demonstrate him, a fundamental reason of contemporary disbelief.

However, the above does not excuse serious defects in expression such as: "the Trinity transcends monotheism." Marcion would be pleased with that. Or again, ". . . unless we made it be, the Kingdom of God shall never come." I recommend that the reader meditate upon the recent little work by von Balthasar: *Zuerst Gottes Reich* (Benziger, 1966) which reconsiders a theological study of the expectation of the *Parousia*—the presence of God—in the consciousness of Christ in the Gospels. Yet Dewart's development with difficulty accords with his affirmations on the infallibility of the Church.

Finally, it seems to us that Dewart confuses the development of theology and the development of dogma. A dogmatic definition does not entail a complete knowledge of the faith—even

41

relatively speaking. It definitely discards an erroneous reading of the Scripture, incompatible with the faith of the Church. Dogma is understood only in the permanent reference of the consciousness of the Church to Scripture. The development of theology should not be limited to an explanation of dogma. Certainly such a past is normative. The consciousness of the Church does not disown her own past. But she situates it precisely as her past to which she must unceasingly address the present with a theology. In a formula too brief to be adequate, we willingly would say that dogma presents itself as "the already" of theology and theology as "the not yet" of dogma.

Therefore, there are very profound reasons for the "weight" of dogma. And one perfectly understands why often councils have proclaimed with regret. On the other hand, the development of theologies is truly a sign of vitality.

We believe that Dewart's stimulating book adds his voice to a concert that begins to be powerful. Let us rejoice in seeing vindicated so strongly the fundamental points upon which contemporary theological research ought to apply itself. And if we are not in agreement, let us set to work to do better than he has.

5.

Must Scholasticism Go?

JAMES F. ANDERSON

THIS QUESTION is vital, not of course because it is new (the sixteenth-century reformers, for instance, replied with a resounding Yes!) but because it is "utterly radical," as Harvey Cox said: it reaches down to the roots. What is this recent, rock-bottom, argument for the abolition of Scholasticism? [1] Seemingly it comes to saying that the indispensable condition of an adequate Christian philosophy is the complete "dehellenization" of its concepts. This cleansing of the stables of Greek ideas must be thorough: no partial purification will do. The conceptual "dehellenization" called for means disposing of the whole machinery of "hellenic" speculation, beginning with the idea of "being." A radical proposal indeed! Of all human notions this is the most basic one. Now in the last analysis, "Scholasticism," it is argued, is but the heir of this "hellenic" speculation—this "Greek metaphysics." Thus the pivotal point of Scholastic thought—the notion of God as the Supreme Being, as He Who Is—proceeds from

1. Cf. Leslie Dewart, *The Future of Belief*. To my knowledge this is the most fundamental and original contemporary presentation. I prescind from detailed criticism in order to concentrate, hopefully, on essentials. The main issue is too important to risk obscuring it by attention to scholarly minutiae.

43

hellenic, not Judaeo-Christian, sources.[2] So too do such ideas as omnipotence, eternity, immutability, analogy, supernature—in short, the total Scholastic lexicon.[3] All this must be discarded as being essentially only an extension of "Greek metaphysics." One asks at once: discarded in favor of what? The answer is: the dynamism of "history," "consciousness," "concreteness," "presence," "actuality," etc.[4]

Excellent things, all these! Are they incompatible with "Greek metaphysics"? Is the latter really disposable? Conceivably it could be were it one thing: systems of thought can be discarded like old suits of clothes. But of course there is no such thing as "Greek metaphysics" in the sense of a single, monolithic, structure: the many hellenic ontologies exhibit little or no conceptually systematic homogeneity. Are not some of them, in fact, irreducibly diverse? "Greek metaphysics" is not disposable in the sense that a system is disposable because it is not a system.

At first sight the entire "dehellenization" argument rests on the mythical supposition of a common "Greek metaphysical tradition" stemming from Parmenides' postulate of the equivalence of being and intelligibility." [5] Need one repeat that history reveals no such "tradition" in the sense of the passing on of a notionally uniform body of knowledge, with some minor variations. Keen "dehellenizers" like Professor Dewart cannot be proposing that! What, then, are they really up to? The thing they have in mind, I suggest, is that the idea of necessity provides a binding link amidst the variety of Greek ontologies. Hellenic necessitarianism, even on the level of cosmology, in fact is ubiquitous. From Parmenides to Aristotle, it plays a commanding role. No Greek thinker ever conceived of the radical contingency

2. *Op. cit.*, pp. 201, 206.
3. *Ibid.*, pp. 189 ff.
4. E.g., *ibid.*, p. 169.
5. *Ibid.*, p. 153.

of finite existents. That is why none of them had a doctrine of creation *ex nihilo*—a conclusion so well established that its documentation would be superfluous. But it is precisely this difference that marks the radical disparity between Greek ontology and Christian existential metaphysics.

True, the Christian philosophers thought that God as the Supreme Being was "necessary." But this necessity meant not that he was some sore of static Essence *á la* Parmenides. (Spinoza's nature-God is much more Parmenidean than that of any of the Scholastics!) Rather, it meant that he was so livingly present that he could not not-be. In short, if a kind of essentialistic immobilism and necessitarianism is charactaristic of much Greek ontology, the opposite is true of Christian metaphysics, even though the latter cannot dispense with the idea of "being," as the "dehellenization" advocates recommend. (Marcel's "presence" is, of course, just *being*-present.)

Even as there is no such thing as "Greek metaphysics" as a single, monolithic system, so there is no "Scholasticism" in that sense. (All potent philosophies are "Scholastic," as they say, by definition: they give rise to "schools"—Hindu, Greek, Western, etc.) But there is, unfortunately, an all-too-real kind of doctrinaire Graeco-Christian scholasticism whose proper name is perhaps "formalism." This indeed must and, it is hoped, will "go."

Now Christian metaphysics of the mistakenly maligned "existential" variety does not conceive of "essence" as the locus of intelligibility *as opposed* to "existence." Indeed, it is rather well known that, according to one brand of Christian "Scholasticism," the former ("essence") is the latter ("existence"), limiting it in creatures, being it in God.

It may be useful to note that there is nothing verbally sacrosanct about the celebrated "real distinction." A Christian philosopher like St. Augustine, for example, doesn't speak in those terms, but in terms of "is not" and "is": God alone is "is"; all else, comparatively, is not.[6] St. Thomas' identification of *essentia* and *esse* in God, with their "real distinction" (or *compositio*) in everything else, means, I think, the same thing. Likewise, the "potency-act" pair is foreign to Augustine's vocabulary, though perhaps not at all to his thought.[7] The point is that the so-called "real distinction" is conceptually indispensable in a world of Christian theism, wherein God is the *Lord* of History—read Process, Evolution, Becoming, Existence—and not just history itself.[8]

To be sure, the God of Christian theism is not the god of any Greek metaphysics. Rather, he is the actual immanent-transcendent Presence. Clearly the latter is but an emphatic name for "Being." (The preceding phrase implies, too, that God is the ubiquitous primary Mind, Consciousness, Personality.) If "being" is an indispensable word in many languages, is it not notionally essential to them all? The question is purely rhetorical.

Undeniably, Christian theism incorporates a good deal of Greek metaphysics and epistemology. This reality ought to elicit from us all both critical acknowledgement and gratitude. Yet it is an illusion to suppose—a truth that Professor Dewart's work vividly demonstrates—that any conceptual lexicon is historically unconditioned. But it is because thought and language are human things that a Western man cannot be fully human without being at least partly "Greek."

Now while these two human things are closely connected in fact, one should beware of assuming conceptual commonness because of verbal identity, or even similarity. Thought and language, though not dichotomized, remain nonetheless unidentified. No

6. Cf. *Confessions*, VII, 11.17; *Commentary on Psalm 134*, 4.
7. E.g., see his *On Christian Doctrine*, I, 32, and *Commentary on St. John's Gospel*, XXVIII, 8. 8–10. Also my monograph *St. Augustine and Being* (Nijhoff, 1965).
8. As Prof. Dewart proposes, *op. cit.*, p. 197.

doubt, Christian philosophers have been too prone to stress the chimera of a separateness between these two aspects of man's socio-cultural life. It is questionable whether any such thinkers, until fairly recent times, adequately appreciated the fact that conceptualization is in large part (I do not say wholly) an historical process by which consciousness evolves.[9] Let us be grateful for such contemporary findings, insights, or emphases. Yet at the same time this hardly warrant's one's blurring the distinction between conceptualization and the tools of its communicability. After all, there *are* translations.

It is perfectly correct to observe, moreover, that "we *cannot* empirically intuit the real indistinction of essence and existence in God."[10] Yet the consequence of this is not, as in Kant, that "our concepts are *in principle* unable to make known to us the actual existence of God."[11] For, thanks to the (often wittily, if nonsensically, rejected) principle of proportional participation, it is possible to infer his utterly underived Presence from contingently existing data of our common experience—notwithstanding the eminent negativity of this knowledge. (Who has not heard the lapidary pronouncement that "we do not know what God is but what he is not, and the relationship of other things to him"?) So, then, since God *is* in his own way, he is known to be accordingly, not indeed by any extension of univocal notions, however inflated, but through analogous ones, irremediably polyvalent and only proportionally similar to their creaturely derivatives. This conclusion may in some true measure

9. E.g., cf. Dewart, *ibid.,* p. 102. However, if genuinely revealed truths did not contain a core of meaning not subject to historical relativity, in the ordinary sense of the term, they would not be universally applicable: their "catholicity" results from, and is guaranteed by, their theistic origin. To cite an eminent instance: the Incarnation is for *all* men.

10. *Ibid.,* p. 158.

11. *Ibid.*

involve "Greek metaphysics," yet it would seem to be substantially inescapable. Indeed, the history of Christian philosophy including some contemporary non-Anglo-Saxons,[12] shows that that point, despite myriad semantical variations, exceeds the scope of linguistics.

Let us agree wholeheartedly on the following desirable rejection. I refer to a kind of pejoratively abstract or formalistic "Scholasticism" operating with homogeneous ideas in a quasi-geometrical mode. Who is not painfully familiar with such a surrogate for genuine thought? This sort of thing is entirely dispensable, its demise to be happily hastened. Nevertheless, may we not also concur in cultivating a Christian metaphysics—an "ontological inquiry"[13]—focused on "reality, concreteness, immediacy, actuality, historicity and factuality"?[14] We can and we must, because the foregoing simply amounts to saying that such a philosophy is *esse*-centered—precisely in the open and humble spirit of St. Thomas himself—not that doctrinaire, archaeological "Thomism" all too commonly practiced and known. This sort of "ontological inquiry"—this "metaphysics of presence"—this "authentic existentialism"—is altogether indispensable.

Notice that the descriptive terms used above—"reality," "concreteness," "immediacy," "actuality," "historicity," "factuality" —all these have more or less analogous correlates in "Greek metaphysics"—developable therefrom, as indeed history shows, but not simply sublatable.

In conclusion let this be said. Professor Dewart and other Christian philosophers are to be thanked for helping us to see more clearly the unique independence of Christian *belief* vis-á-vis all philosophies. For although as philosophers, even Christian

12. See Bibliography of my forthcoming *Reflections on the Analogy of Being* (Nijhoff, 1967).

13. Dewart's description, *ibid.,* p. 169.

14. *Ibid.*

philosophers, we cannot get along without the legacy of the Greeks, however transformed the latter may be, as believers we are not wedded to any particular speculative tradition, Western or Eastern. Yet, insofar as "philosophy" is a communicable wisdom, it cannot dispense with "abstract ideas," even though it be in fact a way of life, and not only of knowledge as some of the Greeks, incidentally, insisted that it is.

6.

Leslie Dewart:
Heretic or Hellene?

FREDERICK WILHELMSEN

A MAN WHO attacks the hellenic heritage of Christianity and
then proceeds to use Aristotelian logic with rigor and even
delicacy is resourceful. Leslie Dewart, in *The Future of Belief*,
has stacked the cards in his favor. His thesis: Catholic Christianity must consciously expunge the Greek mind that it assimilated
in the first flush of the Patristic Age. His advantage: any opponent who uses that same philosophical inheritance in order to
oppose the arguments advanced can be dismissed as having failed
to get the point of the book.

The St. Michael's College (Toronto) professor hammers that
point home early in the game: "today's everyday experience
requires not merely the *demythologization of Scripture* but the
more comprehensive *dehellenization of dogma,* and specifically
that of the Christian doctrine of God." [1] He reminds us of the
point time and again and occasionally pleads for it rhetorically:
"Is there any intrinsic need, due to fidelity to the Christian faith,
to believe that the basic metaphysical notions of the Greek

1. The emphases in quotations are, throughout, Dewart's.

51

philosophical tradition are true?" Dewart grants that hellenization accounted for the brilliant early development of dogma; yet
dogma petrified after the Council of Chalcedon, and Christianity
has had to make do through some fifteen hundred years with an
"underdeveloped" and impoverished doctrinal expression of
faith.

We shall examine this thesis in due course, but a logically
prior matter deserves notice at the outset. *Dewart's entire argument rests on presuppositions that cannot be demonstrated metaphysically, but that can only be advanced rhetorically—by ap-
pealing to experience.* These presuppositions are: Catholic
dogma, as enshrined in the historic creeds, cuts no ice with
modern man and is, in fact, unintelligible to him; the modern
consciousness is superior to all that went before and marks a
coming of age by a civilization that has taken too long to get out
of its swaddling clothes. From these two premises Dewart draws
the obvious conclusion: the Catholic Church must jettison its
doctrines, burdened as they are by an unsophisticated metaphysics, and adjust itself to a secular world which is more adult than
the Church. He carefully warns against interpreting this conclusion merely as a call to a deeper penetration into the content of
doctrine already formulated by the Church; he insists that any
fresh restatement in contemporary symbols of the truths of the
Faith would drain his proposed reform of meaning and interest.
Dewart wants new truths and new doctrines, and he wants them
at the expense of the old ones.

Now these presuppositions are, obviously, open to challenge.
Those of us who have dealt extensively with converts, men and
women drawn to the Church out of the very vortex of contemporary industrial civilization, know that the typical approach to the
Faith involves a *rejection,* even a contempt of the "contemporary
consciousness"—that it is often united with an almost savage
cleaving, not only to the most venerable traditions of the Church,

but even to the peculiarities of that Mediterranean mind Dewart busies himself disparaging.

Dewart can also be challenged for everywhere taking for granted the intellectual and moral superiority of contemporary man over his ancestors without offering one line of evidence. Since his whole case, not for doctrinal *aggiornamento,* which he rejects, but for doctrinal revolution, depends on the supposed superiority of modernity over the past, the witness of those who experience the world quite differently in their daily lives surely ought to be taken into account. It seems strange that a man so fond of Gabriel Marcel has failed to follow his example of never building a philosophical position upon arguments not buttressed by a delicate phenomenology. Not one paragraph in the book, otherwise marked by careful and measured reasoning, is given over to demonstrating, by example or insight, that contemporary man is so mature that he merits from the Church a job of aesthetic surgery upon the very body of her teaching, in order that she might become attractive enough to merit the attention of the truly splendid age in which we live.

In other matters Dewart is quite respectful of "conservatives," crediting them with a practical wisdom not often acknowledged by "liberal" innovators. Therefore his awareness that they are not "the stupid party" ought to have moved him, not through courtesy but through curiosity, to have investigated *their* contention that the only decent reaction to the contemporary experience of the secularized West is that of the young man in Anthony Burgess's novel, *Tremor of Intent,* who "went . . . into a corner," heaved his shoulders, and "tried to throw up the modern world." If those whom Dewart regards as the party of tradition agree with Mr. Michael Lawrence "that the modern world needs to be vomited out of history," it follows that the professor ought to have paused long enough to consider their evaluation of the supposed maturity and superiority of modernity before launching into a program of doctrinal reform whose end is adjustment to this very contemporary consciousness.

In a word, conversation with Dewart cannot center on the way in which he experiences the modern world. On this level we can simply exchange testimonies and let the chips fall where they may. There is a sundering abyss separating those who agree with Eliseo Vivas that it is a mark of decency to be ashamed to have been born in the twentieth century and the Dewarts who hold that our moment in time reflects not a decline, but an advance in consciousness and spirituality. But while a man's evaluation of the secularized West neither supports nor detracts from Dewart's philosophy and theology, from a dialectical point of view, the evaluation is crucial existentially. It is crucial because a sick world—and we radical Christians think that the world is very sick indeed—calls for surgery upon it and not upon the Church it has rejected.

The point is that the *politics* underlying *The Future of Belief* rests upon assumptions that Dewart neither questions nor demonstrates. Most reactions to his book, moreover, will be formed in terms of this politics and not in terms of the philosophy supporting it. Only a fraction of the multitudes being urged today by awed reviewers (Catholics foremost among them) to rush to the nearest bookstore for that blue jacket promising "theism in a world come of age" possess the philosophical training and learning necessary to follow his thesis intelligently.

And yet that thesis is not without interest to philosophy.

I propose in the space available here to do three things with it—(1) summarize the thesis briefly in a way that will familiarize the lay reader with the kind of thing that is recommended in many quarters today as "Catholic" philosophy; (2) suggest a critique of the thesis that evaluates its claims to philosophical novelty, but that presupposes a professional's familiarity and competence to deal with the metaphysical details of Dewart's argument; (3) explain in less technical terms the spectacular failure of the thesis—its failure to grasp the truly radical implications of orthodox Christian metaphysics—and the disastrous consequences to the Faith of seeking radical solutions *outside* of orthodoxy. In warning the layman of the difficulties of Part 2, I mean only to say that the argument there can be bypassed, that it is not essential to an understanding of why Leslie Dewart is either a very backward Catholic philosopher, or is not a Catholic at all.

I

Dewart's central argument is that we must work out a new formulation of our understanding of the nature of truth—one that conforms to modern man's experience of the world. And once we have done that, he concludes, it is clear that we will have to discard traditional dogmas, reinforced by Scholastic philosophy, asserting the Existent, Personal and Trinitarian God of Catholic orthodoxy. The Scholastic synthesis holds, to put the matter briefly, that truth is the conformity of the human intellect to *being*—a relation that is established in the intellectual act of *judgement*. This view, as Dewart is aware, precludes the possibility that "old" truths about revelation may fall into obsolescence and give away to "new" ones. Thus, in order to propound a revolutionary theology, he must first propound a new theory of truth.

Now this task, in turn, requires a new theory of knowledge. According to the Scholastics, knowledge is the intentional act through which a human subject unites himself to an object—an act, put otherwise, through which the intellect unites itself to being. Truth, therefore, is found in the knowing human subject's awareness of his relation to the object in question, to being—an awareness that, since it results from an intentional act, takes the form of a "judgment." Dewart will have none of this because none of it jibes with modern man's more refined understanding of the elements of knowledge. According to Dewart, we can now understand that knowledge is a process through which an initially undifferentiated experience is penetrated and illuminated by the human consciousness. A man's consciousness, moreover, takes the form of *concepts* which are culturally and historically structured. They are so structured because "consciousness is not an essentially original and private event afterwards communicated (through signs) to other human beings"; rather it is a public event from the beginning. For Dewart, the "concept" (or knowledge) is itself *"the cultural form* of human experience."

Having rejected the Scholastic theory of knowledge, and therefore of truth, Dewart is able to advance his own view of truth—namely, that it is located formally within "concepts." Any "concept is true *to the degree* that by its elevation of experience to consciousness it permits the truth of human experience to come into being." Thus he has apparently discovered a "truth" beyond "the truth."

This discovery does not, however, enhance the stature of God. The reduction of all knowledge to concepts has quite the contrary effect.

For Dewart, the Christ of the creeds and the God of Christianity becomes a "presence"—and *merely* "a presence"—perceived in conceptual consciousness in precisely the way in which everything else is perceived by man. The "experience" of God is, to be sure, somewhat different from other experiences. "God is, among other ways in which we can conceptualize the matter, that which we experience as the open background of consciousness and being." God, himself, however, has no being. Therefore, we cannot say that He *is*. We can no longer believe that God *exists*. There is a sense, according to Dewart, in which God is a "reality"; but the sense is so ephemeral that we are advised not to try to give Him a name. In the future, Catholics as well as other "believers" might better worship Him in silence.

II

Dewart's theory of truth is unacceptable to any Thomist. The Thomist holds that truth is never found in concepts at all—and this because of his anti-Platonic conviction that truth is not a meaning or an intelligibility but an existential relation between meanings and things. St. Thomas's teaching that truth is rooted in the very *exercise* of existence caused him to locate the mind's possession of truth in an act—the act that affirms or denies being. Concepts, in Thomistic epistemology, are existentially neutral in the sense that they can be purged of an explicit reference to singular existents in the course of scientific or any other kind of inquiry. Indeed, if the conceptual order did embrace existence, there would be no such thing as an unanswered question.

In propounding his view that truth is found formally within concepts rather than within judgment, Dewart attacks Scholasticism for failing to give an account of error or falsity. A more sophisticated understanding of intentionality would have taught him that false judgments *intend* (in the technical sense) the term of the relation of knowledge *merely as a term.* What exists as an object of knowledge in such cases exists merely and solely as an object and not as a subject of existence. Although the judgment remains relational, in other words, the relation has not been referred to extramental reality. I recommend to Professor Dewart Francis Parker's essay in *The Return to Reason,* "Realistic Epistemology." (Dewart's rejection of the doctrine of intentionality as outmoded is curious; for after falling into disuse for centuries, the doctrine has been revived precisely in the modern age to which Dewart is so anxious to adjust. I think of the reappearance of the doctrine in Husserl's phenomonology, which is traceable to his contacts with Brentano and to the subsequent expansion of an understanding of man as intentionality—some of it illicit in my view—in the existentialism of Heidegger and Sartre.)

Thomistic epistemology, then, reflects a metaphysics of being that inisists upon essence-existence polarity—essence being captured noetically in the conceptual order and the existent being affirmed in judgment. This psychosomatic act implies the marriage of soul and body: although man affirms being through his intellect, he encounters the material world through sensation. Dewart takes issue with this metaphysics on the grounds that the real distinction between essence and being in creatures renders "the *intellect* incompetent for knowing the actual existence of *any* essence, be it created or uncreated." But this is an odd case for the prosecution to lay before the jury because the defendent in question, St. Thomas, has already built *his* whole case around a confession of the very point. Thomistic realism, that is to say, is radically pessimistic about the intelligence being able to know anything at all in isolation from sensation. That the intellect cannot "know" created or uncreated existence (*esse*) is, according to Thomists, both a matter of human experience and a consequence of the abstractive nature of intellection.

But it is also a consequence of something far deeper: the structure of being itself. Dewart seems to be aware of this; he strikes at the Thomistic metaphysics of being with such vigor— apparently because he knows that unless he can discredit it, he cannot reduce truth to the conceptual order and, without doing *that,* he cannot call for a theological revolution. It is instructive to watch our author come to grips with St. Thomas on the meaning of being: Dewart seems sure that he knows what Aquinas was up to. (He even pauses to act as a moderator between

Gilson and Maritain on their reading of the Common Doctor, opting for Maritain.) But that he actually knows a little less than he supposes is clear from the following crucial mistake. Dewart understands Thomas to have based his "real" distinction between existence and essence on the grounds that *"a reflective analysis of our knowledge reveals . . .* in created being a real distinction between" them.

St. Thomas inherited this teaching from Avicenna, and repeated it often; but he was fully aware that it was convincing only in the framework of a metaphysics that conceives of existence as an Aristotelian "accident" added to an already constituted essence. Now since the human mind is, in fact, forced to "conceive" the situation in this way, the argument of Avicenna is useful as an introduction into the deeper meaning of being. St. Thomas's use of Avicenna, however, is little more than a ceremonial bow in the direction of a worthy pioneer. The true distance between Avicenna and Aquinas can be measured only by understanding that for St. Thomas existence is the very act of being, without which there simply are no essences at all—not even in thought. The Thomistic distinction between existence and essence (or better, their "non-identity") is not established by a "reflexive analysis of our knowledge," but through a process of reasoning that distinguishes that-in-the-real through which things *are* from that-in-the-real through which they are *what* they are. If "being X" belonged to the very structure of being, then it would follow that "being" always implies "X." But fidelity to the Many precludes our absorbing them into a monism of being, understood as an undifferentiated ontological block. The Thomistic essence, then, emerges ultimately as "the so much and no more" (Gilson) of an act of existing. Essence is an inner limit posited in being by the existential activity that it structures and determines.

In short, the tail Professor Dewart is wagging is not the Dumb

Ox's at all, but Avicenna's. Which is really not surprising because, as Gilson never tires of repeating, Thomas's revolution in metaphysics was so profound and radical that not even his immediate disciples such as Giles of Rome knew what he was up to.

That the Christian revolution in philosophy has not been grasped by our latter-day revolutionary in dogma, Dr. Dewart, is further evident from the line: "truth cannot remain *the same*. It would make as little sense to say that existence remains *the same*." It is true that existence never "remains the same"—but not for those reasons that forbid a parallel conclusion about truth. Created existence (what I like to call radical extramentality) is neither "the same" *nor* "the other." Both of those concepts are reducible to the quasi-transcendental—what St. Thomas called *aliquid,* and both enjoy only logical existence. When projected out into the real, they are tricks we play on ourselves.

And these tricks lead to bad theology. Dewart's repeated contention, following Luther and Barth, that "God is the Totally Other"—the absolutely Transcendent—reveals a failure to break through to the ultimate frontiers of the real: God is neither "same" nor "other" any more than the created act of existence is reducible to this logical geometry. A wholly "transcendent god" must be defined in terms of the immanence denied him; but that god is obviously not the Catholic God.

Here may be the place to drop some hints (without attempting to elaborate them) as to the direction that a deeper probing of Thomas's teaching on the meaning of existence might take in our day. Before philosophers join Dewart in doing away with "existence" in the name of "facticity" and "presence," they might consider the following propositions:

—Created existence (*esse*) neither is nor is not. (The tradition affirms this by insisting that existence is "non-subsistent" in the creature, but the tradition here truly is burdened by the hellenic mind.)

—Created existence is neither affirmable nor deniable.

—Created existence is neither "the same" nor "the other."

—Created existence is non-identity. Existential Identity is God Himself and the creature encounters its identity in His Being. Ultimately I am not God because I am not my being (*esse*) and because my being (*esse*) is not.

—Created existence is non-contradiction understood as radical extramentality and not as a principle governing the intelligence: i.e., the principle itself of non-contradiction "out there" in the real (the spatial metaphor seems inevitable) *is* the act of existence.

—Created existence is non-cessation which must not be confused with either "the dynamic" or the "static."

—Created existence is not tautological—it cannot be repeated. How could that which neither is nor is not, but without which nothing is at all, be repeated?

—Created existence is neither past, present, nor future; it escapes all three ecstasies of time.

—Created existence is not a "now" or an "already" because it is not a "presence" (*pace* Dewart) at all.

—Created existence is the act of synthesizing the analytic order. By contrast, created essence—through *esse*—is the dynamics of the analytic order. Essence is causality, Aristotle's four causes.

—It follows that created existence is a "plus" or an excessus as St. Thomas teaches (but without exploiting the insight) in *In Divinis Nominibus*. Existence escapes every analytical operation and all concepts. The activity of existence is the "beyond" that is lost the moment we reduce the complexity of the real to its constitutent parts. Existence is what is left behind when the lover

61

ticks off the excellences of his beloved to a friend or to himself; it is that without which she would not be at all.

—Created existence is not a "presence" (sorry about that, Professor Dewart) because it is never given to us in this life. It is interesting that Dewart, having tried to destroy the "correspondence theory of truth" early in his book, eventually returns to a measure of Thomistic good sense by affirming that "the existence of *things* is self-evident." In this case "existence" presumably determines the mind irrespective of "cultural concepts." But this is a shallow Thomism. For it is precisely not "the existence" of things that is self-evident; rather it is "the things" that are evident (although not *self*-evident). Were their existence evident, they would not be.

III

The trouble with Dewart is that he is not radical enough. Having failed to understand how far St. Thomas progressed from Avicenna—and thus that the job of dehellenizing Christian thought was done centuries ago—Dewart has failed utterly to grasp the stupendous implications of Thomas's insights into the structure of being. Some of these implications, indeed, seem to have been hidden from Thomas himself. But they may now serve as a framework for—more, as an urgent invitation to—truly radical explorations into a theology of the future.

Thomas understood that the logical distinction between essence and existence in God, which so fascinates Dewart, is not central to the metaphysics of existence. As he put it in *De Potentia Dei,* the real problem lies elsewhere: "God does not enter the essence of created things, but [nonetheless] their *esse* cannot be understood unless seen as deduced from the divine *Esse.*" This meant that Nature, stripped of its pagan and Greek divinity by Christianity, could now be penetrated without any reference whatever to God. But note that this charter of independence from any metaphysical or theological totalitarianism, granted to science by the Catholic Church with her customary graciousness, is linked paradoxically with an absolute impossibility even to think of existence unless "it" be thought of as "in God." Once the human spirit has cracked the limits of nature and encounters the astounding miracle of being, either God must be affirmed or the spirit must fall into the anguish of existentialist Nothingness. Being elicits our allegiance to God, or being slips away in Heideggerian *Angst.* In no sense do we require—nor is the metaphysician granted—the "presence" of God. God is affirmed to be *without* appearing, and thus without filling the night of the intellect with the Light which is Himself. This misery of metaphysics, in the felicitous phrase of Maritain, might very well be the philosopher's paraphrase of St. John of the Cross (who, however, was dealing with far graver matter): *"y en el monte, nada."* The metaphysician has not found God, and He has not emerged before the philosophical reason either as an object or as a presence. But the philosopher now knows in the darkness of his reason that unless He be, nothing is.

Here is where Dewart misses an opportunity. By insisting that God is merely a "presence," he not only flattens the Christian experience of God, but misses his best chance to build a true theology for the future around the only metaphysical reality that *is* the Future: Christ.

We can approach the issue by meditating on Aristotle's clue to what might be the deepest dilemma in purely human or political life. In the *Rhetoric* the Stagirite suggests that the wise and good man—the statesman annealed in philosophical truth—can never propose the *being* of moral excellence (*arete*) to the populace because the populace, not possessing this virtue, will never understand the philosopher. The philosopher must be content with suggesting what goodness will *do* for the community rather than what it *is*. Behind Aristotle's pessimism lies a truly deep understanding of the nature of the political act. Belonging as it must to the future (there are no political acts with consequences in the past), the political, or human, act is addressed to what is not. The future has not yet been determined, and hence cannot be said to exist. This is true of every future except the only Future that is: Christ, "The Fullness of Time."

In the words of St. John the Evangelist: "We are now the sons of God; and it hath not yet appeared what we shall be. We know that, when He shall appear, we shall be like Him because we shall see Him as He is." Our very personalities are *not* discovered through conceptual consciousness and are *not* "emergent" in experience as Dewart imagines, but will be revealed to us only when we confront our future who is the Incarnate God. Dewart holds forth the prospect for man's future of a "beyond personality"; but this "beyond" truly *is* the Person in whom I find my own identity, who in truth *is* that Identity. In his fondness for Teilhard de Chardin's evolutionary Omega Point (our author has the good sense to caution against some of the French Jesuit's philosophical weaknesses), Dewart misses the utter radicalness of Christianity's teaching on the future. Anybody who builds a theology around an emergence from the past, no matter how "cosmic" it might be, anyone who seeks Christ *there,* is simply backing out of the present into the future with his gaze transfixed on the past. This is certainly not a theology for tomorrow, whatever else it might be.

Dewart and those who think as he does would *determine* our encounter with Christ by adjusting the Church, His Mystical Body, to a secular eschatology masking itself as maturity, and to an already dead secular way of life. This is sheer reaction; it fails utterly to grasp the *absolute* liberty that the radical Christian senses. The secularized world has already come into being. Thus it is a past to me as I stand at the crossroads of time. It cannot determine my future, and I owe it not the slightest allegiance. It rejects both the liberty of man and his being in the Person of Christ, his only tomorrow. The world to which Dewart would adjust God can be wiped away with all the astonishing absoluteness with which sin is annihilated in the confessional. A theology of the future transcends this world or it is nothing.

The openness, the fullness, the "futureness" of God also escapes Dewart in his discussion of the Trinity, which, he fears, the modern Christian will have to do without. "Christian theism might in the future not conceive God as a person—or indeed as a Trinity of persons." Dewart is dissatisfied with the orthodox understanding of the divine "processions" in terms of a triune personhood. The Christian tradition is alleged to have treated God as an Aristotelian first cause to which it later attached, as a kind of afterthought, three persons. By building these metaphysical "blocks," theologians tricked believers into an implicit tritheism. However, as I have written elsewhere: "Every community of nature grows itself out of the ecstasy of personality . . . God, for the patristic mind . . . is a personal and *hence* self-giving Act: this Act, an infinite ecstasy and fecundity, is expressed within Himself in the Trinity and beyond in the act of creation. The priority of personality over nature caused the Greek Fathers to approach the mystery of the Holy Trinity from a point of view which differs from that of the Latins. Whereas the Latins began with Unity of the Divine Nature and attempted to understand the Three Persons in the light of that unity, the Greeks began with the three persons and saw the Unity of Nature in the light of the Trinity of Persons. Their eminently personalistic theology was made possible by a theology of the real that saw the ultimate meaning of being in *agape*, in ecstasy as rooted precisely in God as personal, as superabundant." [2]

2. *The Metaphysics of Love*, 1962.

The Trinitarian structure of being, adumbrated in this life in the family, where the very existence of the child grows out of a "we," implies an understanding of personality which is one with *agape,* with what St. John Damascene called "superabundance." This law of unity in variety and variety in unity is regarded by Donoso Cortés as the fundamental law of being. Chesterton did not hesitate to call God a "holy company," and we do well to remember his terrible line: "We Trinitarians have known that it is not good for God to be alone."

Not surprisingly, Dewart's perverse view of the future also moves him to relieve God of authority—concretely, His superiority over men. For the notion of "superiority" belongs to those wicked "hierarchical relations" from which modern man has been emancipated. Modern man, then, is not only clearly superior to all of the men who went before him; he can now look even his Creator straight in the eye. And so God slinks down the road of the "future" and slips out of history. It is a dreary end for two thousand years of Christian history; it would be pleasing to know that God were not a person, and so could be spared this impudence.

What, in fine, are we to make of a talented Catholic scholar who finishes off an attack on traditional Catholic philosophy by stripping God (all the while piously insisting on the tentativeness of such conclusions) of His authority, His personality, His Trinity, His very being—much as a bemused child finishes undressing a doll by twisting off its head? First, suspect the protestations of tentativeness: the sincere man who is merely tempted by heresies is not likely to write a book aimed at the bestseller lists explaining their plausibility. Second, give the man the benefit of the doubt; give him a chance to explain how the "reality" of God in which he professes belief can be reconciled to reducing God to "experience," to an "open background of consciousness and being." It would seem that only two gambits are open: either "reality," as attributed to God, means the experience of God and nothing else; or "reality" somehow stands behind being as an ultimate ontological principle. If Dewart goes with the first possibility, then he is formally an atheist in the sense the Catholic Church understands the term; moreover, he has not escaped the charge of modernism, his protestations to the contrary notwithstanding. If he goes with the second, he has fallen back into the very hellenism he would discard. The idea that "reality" is a radical background to "being" is precisely the teaching of Avicenna, who distorted his own intuitions, having at hand nothing more than the old bottle of Greek essentialism into which to pour the wine of a creationist doctrine of being. That Dewart rejects the term "essence" matters not at all. Once "the real" is allowed to be more profound than being, the intelligence is beset with the contradiction of an ontological zone—call it "open background," "presence," whatever—that somehow is before it is. The only escape from the contradiction is semantic.

But there remains the fact of the book, and of its enthusiastic reception in Catholic circles. As I put down *The Future of Belief* I wondered how young untrained Catholics might react to the book and to its reception. I was gripped by an icy vision of a future "human church," bare, stripped of homage and of all comeliness, bereft of hierarchy and order, its temples emptied of beauty and swept clean of grandeur. In my vision the faith had gone out of the Church, and God had altogether departed. This church blindly worshipped a blind idol called Man. But then I shook off my vision as a bad dream unworthy of the hope that fires men who look to a Future called Christ.

67

7.

The Dehellenization of Dogma

BERNARD J. F. LONERGAN, S.J.

WITH CONSIDERABLE WARMTH Prof. Leslie Dewart appeals to Pope John's decision "to adopt a historical perspective: to 'look to the present, to new conditions and new forms of life . . . to dedicate ourselves with an earnest will and without fear to that work which our era demands of us'" (p. 172). This decision, he feels, and the unhesitating acclamation that greeted it reversed a policy that had been gaining strength for centuries. "This policy was, for the sake of protecting the truth and purity of the Christian faith, to resist the factual reality, and to deny the moral validity, of the development of man's self-consciousness, especially as revealed in cultural evolution" (p. 172).

His purpose, then, is "to sketch an approach to . . . the problem of integrating Christian theistic belief with the everyday experience of contemporary man" (p. 7). He aims at "the integration of Christian belief with the post-medieval stage of human development" (p. 15). He understands contemporary experience "as the mode of consciousness which mankind, if not as a whole at least in respect of our own civilization constituting man's cultural vanguard, has reached as a result of its historical and evolutionary development. And the integration in question must be a true organic process of coordination, interrelation and unification" (p. 9). What is at stake is the unity and coherence of Christian and, in particular, Catholic consciousness: ". . . the problem is, at its most basic level, whether one can, while complying with the demand that human personality, character and experience be inwardly integrated, at one and the same time profess the Christian religion *and* perceive human nature and everyday reality as contemporary man typically does" (p. 19).

So much for the problem. The suggested solution is "that the integration of theism with today's everyday experience requires not merely the *demythologization of Scripture* but the more comprehensive *dehellenization of dogma,* and specifically that of the Christian doctrine of God" (p. 49). Demythologization integrates no more than the Christian's *reading of Scripture* with his contemporary everyday experience; and it creates several dogmatic problems for each scriptural one it solves (p. 47). To go to the root of the matter, to become both coherent and contemporary, we have to transcend our Hellenic past and consciously to fashion the cultural form which Christianity requires now for the sake of its future. So "dehellenization means, in positive terms, the conscious creation of the future of belief" (p. 50). This future, he feels, is likely to depend on whether Christian theism "chooses to contribute to the heightening of man's self-understanding and to the perfection of his 'education to reality.' This would in turn imply that Christian theism should first become conscious that its traditional form has necessarily and logically been childish and infantile to the very degree that it corresponded to an earlier, relatively childish, infantile stage of human evolution. Theism in a world come of age must itself be a theism come of age" (p. 51).

I

The principal means for dehellenizing dogma and obtaining a mature theism seems to be "the theory of knowledge assumed here" (p. 168 n.). While its precise nature is not disclosed in any detail, apparently it involves a rather strong repugnance to propositional truth in some at least of its aspects.

In the theory of knowledge suggested here human knowledge is not the bridging of an original isolation but, on the contrary, the self-differentiation of consciousness in and through its objectification (of the world and of itself); and conceptualization is the sociohistorical mechanism through which the self-differentiation can take place. Concepts are not the *subjective* expression of an *objective* reality (nor, therefore, a means whereby we become reflectively conscious of a self which already existed prior to reflection). Concepts are the self-expression of consciousness and, therefore, the means by which we objectify (the world and the self), and the means by which we self-communicate with another self (including God), that is, the means by which we objectify ourselves for another self, and by which we objectify ourselves for ourselves. [p. 116 n.; here and elsewhere italics in text]

Hence we are repeatedly warned against the view that truth involves an *adaequatio intellectus et rei*.

Truth is not the adequacy of our representative operations, but the adequacy of our conscious existence. More precisely, it is the fidelity of consciousness to being. [p. 92]
It is the result of the mind coming-into-being through the self-differentiation of that-which-is into self and world. [p. 93]
Now we have seen that . . . truth can be understood as an existential relation of self to being which must by definition develop in order

71

to realize itself—and not as the relation of conformity to an objective thing which must by definition be stable in order to be at all. [p. 97]

Although truth is not the adequation of the *intellect* to *being* . . . truth might nevertheless be called an adequation of *man* to *reality*, in the sense that it is *man's self-achievement* within the requirements of *a given situation*. . . . In this context *adequation* would not connote *conformity, correspondence, likeness* or *similarity*. It would connote *adjustment, usefulness, expediency, proficiency, sufficiency* and *adaptation*. [p. 110]

The truth of human experience is the result of consciousness' incessant tending towards being—a tendency which, far from satisfied by the achievement of its goal, is further intensified by whatever success it may meet. Hence, the only valid "criterion" of truth is that it create the possibility of more truth. [p. 111]

. . . the concept is true *to the degree* that by its elevation of experience to consciousness it permits the truth of human experience to come into being. [p. 113]

. . . the concepts in which Christian belief are cast are true, not in virtue of their representative adequacy, but in virtue of their efficacious adequacy as generative forms of the truth of religious experience. [p. 113]

To conclude with a citation from Maurice Blondel's *Carnets intimes:* ". . . truth is no longer the *adaequatio rei et intellectus*. . . . But truth remains, and this truth that remains is living and active. It is the *adaequatio mentis et vitae*" (p. 118).

Prof. Dewart's grounds for his view on truth seem to be partly the flood of light he has derived from phenomenological and existential thought and partly the inadequacy of his interpretation of Scholasticism.

To the light I have no objection. I would not deny that the authenticity of one's living, the probity of one's intellectual endeavors, the strategy of one's priorities are highly relevant for the truth by which one is truly a man. I have no doubt that concepts and judgments (on judgments I find Dewart strangely silent) are the expression of one's accumulated experience, developed understanding, acquired wisdom; and I quite agree that such expression is an objectification of one's self and of one's world. I would urge, however, that this objectification is intentional. It consists in acts of meaning. We objectify the self by meaning the self, and we objectify the world by meaning the world. Such meaning of its nature is related to a meant, and what is meant may or may not correspond to what in fact is so. If it corresponds, the meaning is true. If it does not correspond, the meaning is false. Such is the correspondence view of truth, and Dewart has managed to reject it without apparently adverting to it. So eager has he been to impugn what he considered the Thomist theory of knowledge that he overlooked the fact that he needed a correspondence view of truth to mean what he said.

Let me stress the point. Dewart has written a book on the future of belief. Does he mean the future of belief, or something else, or nothing at all? At least, when he asserts that God is not a being, he assures us that what his statement "means is literally what it says, that God is not a being at all" (p. 175). Again, he wants his proposals tried by the touchstone of public examination (p. 50). But what is that examination to be? What can the public do but consider what he means and try to ascertain how much of what he says is certainly or probably true or false?

Dewart urges that the correspondence view of truth supposes what is contrary to both logic and observation, "as if we could witness from a third, 'higher' viewpoint, the union of two lower things, object and subject" (p. 95). But such a statement is involved in a grave confusion. The witnessing from a higher viewpoint is the nonsense of naive realism, of the super-look that looks at both the looking and the looked-at. On the other hand, the union of object and subject is a metaphysical deduction from the fact of knowledge, and its premise is the possibility of consciousness objectifying not only itself but also its world.

Again, Dewart urges that a correspondence view of truth implies an immobility that precludes development (p. 95) and, in particular, the development of dogma (p. 109). Now I would not dispute that a woodenheaded interpretation of the correspondence view of truth can exclude and has excluded the possibility of development. But that is no reason for rejecting the correspondence view along with its misinterpretation. Least of all is that so at present, when "hermeneutics" has become a watchword and the existence of literary forms is generally acknowledged. For the root of hermeneutics and the significance of literary forms lie precisely in the fact that the correspondence between meaning and meant is itself part of the meaning and so will vary with variations in the meaning.

Just as he discusses truth without adverting to hermeneutics, so Dewart discusses the development of dogma without adverting to the history of dogma. But the development of dogma is a historical entity. Its existence and its nature are determined by research and interpretation. Moreover, on this approach there are found to be almost as many modes of development, almost as many varieties of implicit revelation, as there are different dogmas, so that a general discussion of the possibility of cultural development, such as Dewart offers, can provide no more than philosophic prolegomena.

Unfortunately, it seems of the essence of Dewart's prolegomena to exclude the correspondence view of truth. Such an exclusion is as destructive of the dogmas as it is of Dewart's own statements. To deny correspondence is to deny a relation between meaning and meant. To deny the correspondence view of truth is to deny that, when the meaning is true, the meant is what is so. Either denial is destructive of the dogmas.

If there is no correspondence between meaning and meant, then, in Prof. McLuhan's phrase, it would be a great mistake to read the dogmas as if they were saying something. If that is a great mistake, it would be another to investigate their historical origins, and a third to talk about their development.

If one denies that, when the meaning is true, then the meant is what is so, one rejects propositional truth. If the rejection is universal, then it is the self-destructive proposition that there are no true propositions. If the rejection is limited to the dogmas, then it is just a roundabout way of saying that all the dogmas are false.

II

The same view of truth is applied not only to the dogmas but also to faith and revelation. We are told that "belief must bear directly upon the reality of God, not upon words or concepts" (p. 167). In a footnote we are warned against the doctrine of St. Thomas which has faith terminating at God Himself through the mediation of the propositions of the Creed. Dewart holds that to believe in God by believing a proposition about God is to believe in a proposition and not to believe in God. But this follows only on Dewart's assumption that truth is not correspondence. On the contrary assumption, to assent to the truth of the proposition does not differ from assenting to what the proposition means. *Verum est medium in quo ens cognoscitur.*

With faith detached from assent to propositions (p. 167), it has to be ontic rather than ontological (p. 136 n.).

Faith is the existential response of the self to the openness of the transcendence disclosed by conscious experience. It is our decision to respect, to let be, the contingency of our being, and, therefore, to admit into our calculations a reality beyond the totality of being. It is a lived response, identical with our freely willing to exist in a certain self-conception and self-resolution. . . . It is no less a coming-

75

into-being than the "act" of existence which is, likewise, a perpetual achieving of the unachieved. In real life we find not the act but the life of faith. [pp. 64 f.]

Such faith seems to coincide with religious experience. This differs from ordinary knowledge inasmuch as it is an experience of a transcendent reality first adumbrated negatively in the empirical apprehension of the contingency of our own being. So it is a conscious experience of something inevident, something which unlike this desk and this chair is not seen to be there, even if it enters into the fabric of our personal relations to reality with at least as much force, relevance, and moment as things which are seen to be there. Further, in the traditional phrase, faith is due to God's initiative. Again, faith as Christian is faith as conceptualized under some or other cultural form of the Christian tradition. Its continuity in truth requires the continuity of God's self-communication to man, and the continuity of man's correlative religious experience in response to God's initiative. But this is not the continuity of sameness or the continuity of that which remains (substantially) unchanged in the midst of accidental change. Truth cannot remain the same. It would make as little sense as to say that existence remains the same, that one moment of consciousness is the same as another, or that life is the same thing over and over again (pp. 113–16).

Correlative to faith is revelation:

. . . although God does not reveal propositions or formulae or concepts about himself, he truly reveals himself. . . . He does it personally, by his own agency, through his personal presence to human history, in which he freely chooses to appear and to take part. . . . His revelation to man in the Judaeo-Christian tradition is unique and extraordinary: the Christian religion and the Catholic Church are, in this extraordinary and unique sense, the true religion and the true Church to which all men are called. [p. 115 n.]

76

Dewart, however, does not seem to consider that the call to the true Church calls for some attention to the pronouncements of Vatican I and II on revelation and faith. Instead we have the caricature of a "popular faith" in which "revelation has indeed tended to become God's transmission of cryptic messages. Correlatively, the magisterium of the Church has tended to become the decoding of these messages, and faith the Christian's assent to the accuracy of the translation . . ." (p. 165 n.).

No doubt, Dewart's esotericism is inevitable, once the mediating role of propositions has been eliminated both from God's revelation to man and from man's faith in God. But if one is inclined to doubt the soundness of the "theory of knowledge assumed here" (p. 168 n.), if one's modernity includes a greater interest in exegesis and history than is exhibited in the opinion that "Christianity has a mission not a message" (p. 8), then one will find abundant evidence from New Testament times right up to the present day that the Church has been explicitly aware not only of a mission but also of a message. Moreover, while it is true that the message can be and has been abused to the detriment both of living faith and of the transcendent Revealer, such an abuse does not show that a rejection of the message is not also a rejection of the mission.

III

Prof. Dewart dislikes the Greeks. He deplores the "inability of Hellenic metaphysical thinking to discern *reality* except in *ens*, that-which-is" (p. 180). He places at the sad root of both Greek and Scholastic thought Parmenides' postulate that "that which can be thought is identical with that which can be" (p. 153). He would get beyond "speculative-ideological metaphysics" (p. 163) and establish a metaphysics of presence (p. 169). Then we could get along without the training and education that only relatively few can afford. "Christian theology and philosophy would then cease to be 'academic' subjects, and theological enquiry would once again take place predominantly within the public, everyday, real life of the whole Church" (p. 145 n.). In anticipation of this imminent utopia, he notes that "there is no need, if we discard Parmenides, to make God fit in the mould of being" (p. 176). Hence, he desires a philosophy concerned with the presence and reality of God, a God that is not even partially the God of Greek metaphysics (p. 170). Similarly, he suggests that Christian theology is not to assume any fundamental principle or essential part of that very mode of philosophizing on which was erected the concept of God which can no longer be integrated with contemporary experience (p. 41).

This hostility to Hellenism is of a piece with the already noted hostility to propositional truth; for not only do propositions mediate reality, but also the first-level propositions that do so may be themselves mediated by second-level propositions. So dictionaries speak of words, grammars of languages, logics of the clarity, coherence, and rigor of discourse, hermeneutics of the relation between meaning and meant, and, to come to the villain, metaphysics of what is meant. Such second-level mediation of the first-level mediator was the secret of the Greek miracle that effected the triumph of *logos* over *mythos*.

Obviously, then, if one does not want a first-level mediation of reality by propositions, much less will one tolerate the second-level mediation associated with Greek metaphysics. Moreover, if one does not care to be entirely cut off from reality, one will have to turn to some nonpropositional mode of access such as presence. So Dewart praises a metaphysics of presence but blames a Hellenic metaphysics.

Again, the Greek miracle had its price. It demanded a second differentiation of consciousness, a second withdrawal from the world of immediacy. In that world of immediacy the infant lives, but when the child learns to talk, he also learns to inhabit the far larger world mediated by meaning. For the student, however, there is the further learning that mediates the mediator, that reflects on articulate sounds to correlate them with an alphabet, that uses dictionaries, that studies grammars and logics, that introduces hermeneutics and even perhaps metaphysics. The basic purpose of this further learning is to control the mediation of reality by meaning, to hold in check the affect-laden images that even in the twentieth century have the power to make myth seem convincing and magic seem efficacious.

But however beneficial, the second differentiation of consciousness is onerous. It is all the more onerous, all the more resented, when compulsory, universal education attempts to extend to all what once had to be endured by but few. So the word "academic" acquires a pejorative sense that expresses disapproval of any cultural superstructure. Despite his devotion to the mode of consciousness reached by man's cultural vanguard (p. 9), Dewart feels free to appeal to that disapproval and to look forward to the day when Christian philosophy and theology will no longer be "academic" subjects (p. 145 n.).

A similar ambiguity appears in Dewart's attitude to science. On the one hand, he assures us that "modern man creates himself by means of science, that is, by means of his scientific mode of consciousness," and "it is *scientific culture* that defines *contemporary man*" (p. 18). On the other hand, he is all for discarding Parmenides' identification of the possible object of thought with possible being (pp. 153, 165, 168, 174, 176, 181, 184). But to attack this identification is also to attack a cardinal point in contemporary science; for what is defined by a hypothesis is a possible object of thought, and what is to be ascertained by verification is a real state of affairs. But modern science demands that every hypothesis be verifiable, and so it demands that its hypothetical objects of thought be possible beings. Not only is it thoroughly committed to the Parmenidean identity, but also it has so extended and developed the second differentiation of consciousness as to erect a cultural superstructure far more elaborate and far more abstruse than anything attempted by the Greeks or the Scholastics.

One begins to suspect that Dewart is not a reformer but just a revolutionary. He is dealing with a very real and very grave problem. He would have written an extremely important book, if he had distinguished between the achievements and the limitations of Hellenism, if he had listed the ways in which modern culture has corrected the errors and so transcended the limitations of its ancient heritage, if he had pointed out the precise bearing of each of these advances on each of the many levels on which Christians live and Christianity functions. He has not done so. He fails to discern the elements of Hellenism that still survive in the cultural vanguard, and so he plumps for vigor. Let's liquidate Hellenism. He does not distinguish between integrated consciousness and undifferentiated consciousness, and so he thinks and talks and prescribes his remedies as if prayer, dogma, systematic theology, philosophy, and contemporary common sense were or should be a single homogeneous unity.

IV

Prof. Dewart conceives the development of the Trinitarian and Christological dogmas to have been a matter of taking over Hellenic concepts for the expression of Christian doctrine; for he feels "it would be unhistorical to suppose that at the first moment of the development of Christian consciousness this consciousness could have created the concepts whereby to elaborate itself—it is not until our own day that such a possibility has begun to emerge" (p. 136). Further, he laments that the Church still retains such outworn tools, for today this results in a crypto-tritheism (p. 147) and in a crypto-docetism (p. 152).

It is, I should say, quite unhistorical to suppose that the development of Catholic dogma was an effort of Christian consciousness to elaborate, not the Christian message, but Christian consciousness. Further, it is unhistorical to suppose that Greek philosophy supplied all the principal elements in which we have for centuries conceptualized the basic Christian beliefs of the Trinity and the Incarnation (cf. *America,* Dec. 17, 1966, p. 801). My first contention needs no elaboration, and so I turn to the second.

It is true, then, that profound affinities may be discerned between Hellenic thinkers and some ecclesiastical writers. The Stoic notion that only bodies are real seems intrinsic to Tertullian's account of the divinity of the Son in his *Adversus Praxean.* Middle Platonism is prominent in Origen's account of the Son in his *De principiis* and *In Ioannem.* But the subordinationism of these two writers, along with Arianism, was rejected at Nicaea. Moreover, the term enshrining that rejection was *homoousios,* and while one might speculate that here if anywhere one has a concept forged by deep Hellenic thought and simply taken over by the bishops at Nicaea (see p. 136), it happens that historical research does not justify such a view. According to G. Prestige (*God in Patristic Thought* [London, 1936], p. 209; cf. p. 197), down to the Council of Nicaea *homoousios* was understood in one sense and in one sense only: it meant "of one stuff"; and as applied to the Divine Persons, it conveyed a metaphor drawn from material objects. The Fathers at Nicaea, then, did not find ready to hand a sharply defined, immutable concept which they made into a vehicle for the Christian message; on the contrary, they found a word which they employed in a metaphorical sense.

It may be urged, however, that the metaphor meant something

81

and that meaning must be some other Hellenic concept. It happens, however, that while the metaphor had a meaning, still the meaning was determined not by some Hellenic concept but by a Hellenic technique. What *homoousios* meant exactly, was formulated by Athanasius thus: *eadem de Filio quae de Patre dicuntur, excepto Patris nomine.* The same meaning has been expressed in the Trinitarian Preface: *Quod enim de tua gloria, revelante te, credimus, hoc de Filio tuo, hoc de Spiritu sancto, sine differentia discretionis sentimus.* Now such a determination of meaning is characteristically Hellenic. It is a matter of reflecting on propositions. It explains the word "consubstantial" by a second-level proposition to the effect that the Son is consubstantial with the Father, if and only if what is true of the Father also is true of the Son, except that only the Father is Father.

Let me add five observations on this typically Hellenic technique. The first is that it offers an open structure: it does not determine what attributes are to be assigned to the Father and so must be assigned to the Son as well; it leaves the believer free to conceive the Father in scriptural, patristic, medieval, or modern terms; and of course contemporary consciousness, which is historically minded, will be at home in all four.

The second is that, when reality and being are contrasted, the technique decides for being; for being is that which is; it is that which is to be known through the true proposition; and the technique operates on true propositions. On the other hand, reality, when contrasted with being, denotes the evident or present that provides the remote grounds for rationally affirming being, but, unlike being, is in constant flux.

The third is that specifically Christian thought on being came into prominent existence in Athanasius' struggle against Arianism and, in particular, in his elucidation of *natum non factum,* of the difference between the Son *born* of the Father and the creature *created* by Father and Son. No doubt, such an explanation presupposes a Hellenic background for its possibility. But the problem and the content are specifically Christian. A divine Son was simply a scandal to the Hellenist Celsus; and the Christian notion of creation is not to be found in Plato or Aristotle, the Stoics or the Gnostics. When Dewart talks about the God of Greek metaphysics (p. 170), one wonders what Greek metaphysician he is talking about.

My fourth observation is that the Hellenic technique of second-level propositions is not outworn. The modern mathematician reflects on his axioms and pronounces them to be the implicit definitions of his basic terms. This technique, then, pertains not to the limitations of Hellenism antiquated by modern culture but to the achievements of Hellenism that still survive in modern culture and, indeed, form part of it.

My fifth and last observation is that the technique is not within everyone's competence. The matter seems to have been settled with some accuracy; for, in his celebrated studies of educational psychology, Jean Piaget has concluded that only about the age of twelve (if my memory is correct) do boys become able to operate on propositions. It follows that other means have to be found to communicate the doctrine of Nicaea to less-developed minds. So much for my five observations.

For Dewart, "person" is a concept taken over from Hellenic thought and, though we have not managed to improve on it, we must do so (pp. 143 f.). I find this a rather inadequate account of the matter.

For Augustine, *persona* or *substantia* was an undefined, heuristic concept. He pointed out that Father, Son, and Spirit are three. He asked, three what? He remarked that there are not three Gods, three Fathers, three Sons, three Spirits. He answered that there are three persons or substances, where "person" or "substance" just means what there are three of in the Trinity (*De trin.* 7, 4, 7 [*PL* 42, 939]). Obviously, such an account of the

83

notion of "person" does no more than indicate, so to speak, the area to be investigated. It directs future development but it cannot be said to impede it. The only manner in which it could become outworn would be the rejection of the Trinity; for as long as the Trinity is acknowledged, there are acknowledged three of something.

Moreover, the original heuristic structure, while it has remained, has not remained indeterminate. It has been developed in different ways at different times. There was the stage of definitions, indeed, of the three main definitions contributed by Boethius, Richard of St. Victor, and Thomas Aquinas. There was the Trinitarian systematization that conceived the three Persons as subsistent relations and based the relations upon psychologically conceived processions. If I may cite my own views, I have maintained not only in my classes but also in a textbook that the three Persons are the perfect community, not two in one flesh, but three subjects of a single, dynamic, existential consciousness. On the other hand, I am of the opinion that the Christological systematization, from Scotus to de la Taille, had bogged down in a precritical morass. For the past thirty years, however, attention has increasingly turned to the consciousness of Christ, and my own position has been that the doctrine of one person with two natures transposes quite neatly into a recognition of a single subject of both a divine and a human consciousness.

I may be more brief on such terms as *substantia, hypostasis, natura.* All three were ambiguous. We have just seen Augustine use *substantia* in the same sense as *persona,* a usage that had vanished by the time the *Quicumque vult* was composed. Next, in the *Tomus ad Antiochenos* there is the account of Athanasius reconciling those that argued for one hypostasis with those that argued for three; he asked the former if they agreed with Sabellius, and the latter if they were tritheists; both groups were astounded by the question put them, promptly disclaimed respectively Sabellianism and tritheism, and dropped their now obviously verbal dispute. "Nature," finally, which for Aristotle meant either the form or the matter, and the form rather than the matter, meant neither of these to Christians some eight centuries later. They, however, had their own ambiguous usage, and it was recognized solemnly and explicitly in the sixth and seventh centuries. In successive canons Constantinople II explained the correct meaning both of Chalcedon's two natures and of Cyril's one nature (*DS* 428 f.). More abruptly, Lateran I imposed both the Cyrillian and the Chalcedonian formulas (*DS* 505 f.).

So much for the process of Hellenizing Christian doctrine. Let us add a few words on the meaning of the technical terms; for Dewart roundly asserts that no Christian believer today (unless he can abstract himself from contemporary experience) can intelligently believe that in the one hypostasis of Jesus *two* real natures are united (p. 150). Let me put the prior question. Does Dewart's Christian believer today accept the positive part of the Nicene decree, in which neither the term "hypostasis" nor the term "nature" occurs? If so, in the part about Jesus Christ, does he observe two sections, a first containing divine predicates, and a second containing human predicates? Next, to put the question put by Cyril to Nestorius, does he accept the two series of predicates as attributes of *one and the same* Jesus Christ? If he does, he acknowledges what is meant by one hypostasis. If he does not, he does not accept the Nicene Creed. Again, does he acknowledge in the one and the same Jesus Christ both divine attributes and human attributes? If he acknowledges both, he accepts what is meant by two natures. If he does not, he does not accept the Nicene Creed.

What is true is that Catholic theology today has a tremendous task before it, for there are very real limitations to Hellenism that have been transcended by modern culture and have yet to be successfully surmounted by Catholic theology. But that task is not helped, rather it is gravely impeded, by wild statements based on misconceptions or suggesting unbelief.

V

Prof. Dewart has treated many other topics besides those I have been able to mention, but his principal concern, no doubt, is "theism in a world come of age," for that is the subtitle of his book. The substance of his proposal here seems to come in two parts. Positively, it is that God is to be thought of, not as being or as existing, but as a reality that at times is present and at times is absent (pp. 173 ff.). Negatively, it is that atheism is fostered by unsuccessful efforts to prove God's existence, and such failures are due to the real distinction between essence and existence (pp. 156–58).

He contends, then, that one need not conceive God as being, once one gets beyond the metaphysical method grounded on Parmenides' identity. Remove that method, and "being" need no longer be identified with that-which-is. So the way is opened to giving to "being" a new meaning, and this new meaning is to be found in man. It is because he is present to himself as object that man is most truly a being; for through that presence man may transcend the subjectivity of mere objects and the objectivity of mere subjects to reach an understanding of himself as being. But to associate being with man is to disassociate being from God. As God is simply beyond man, so He is simply beyond being (pp. 173–75). By the same token, God cannot be said to exist (p. 176). He cannot because to exist is proper to being (p. 180).

We are reassured immediately, however, that the denial of being and existence to God takes away nothing of His reality and presence. To exist and to be present are quite different things. A man could be in the same room sitting beside me without being present to me, without making his presence felt. Conversely, God's real presence to us (and, therefore, His reality "in Himself") does not depend upon His being a being or an object. On the contrary, to postprimitives a reality beyond the totality of being reveals itself by its presence (pp. 176 f.).

I do not find this very satisfactory. First of all, Dewart's views on truth are not defensible. Moreover, the cultural vanguard has not yet surmounted the requirement that hypotheses be verifiable, and so Parmenides' identity still stands. It follows that "being" still is that-which-is, that intelligence still is related to reality, that "is" and "is not" are not open to reinterpretation, and that there do not exist the premises for the conclusion that "being" and "existing" are appropriate only to creatures.

Secondly, it is obvious that a person can exist without making his presence felt and that he cannot make his presence felt without existing and being present. But it is also obvious that one can have the feeling that someone is present when no one is there. Especially in a world come of age such feelings should be examined, scrutinized, investigated. The investigation may result in the judgment that someone really is there. It may result in the judgment that really no one is there. It may result only in an unresolved state of doubt. But in any case, what is decisive is not the felt presence but the rational judgment that follows upon an investigation of the felt presence.

My point here is that man's coming to know is a process, that the earlier stages of the process pertain to knowing without constituting it completely, that in each instance of coming to know it is only with the rational act of judgment that the process reaches its term. Dewart does not want propositional truth and so he does not want "being" or "existing" or "that-which-is" or assent to propositions or judgments issuing in propositions. He does very much want the reassuring sense of present reality that can be savored in the earlier phases of cognitional process and, I have no doubt, is to be savored all the more fully if the unpleasant and tiring business of questions, investigations, and possible doubts is quietly forgotten. But this seems to be less "coming of age" than infantile regression.

Thirdly, maturity is comprehensive. It does not refuse to acknowledge any part of man but embraces all from the entities of Freud's psychic embryology to the immanent norms of man's intellectual, rational, existential consciousness. As it does not deny propositional truth, so it does not disregard or belittle religious experience. On the contrary, it is quite ready to claim with Karl Rahner that a mystagogy will play a far more conspicuous role in the spirituality of the future (*Geist und Leben* 39 [1966] 335), and it is fully aware that spiritual advance brings about in prayer the diminution and at times the disappearance of symbols and concepts of God. Still, this differentiation and specialization of consciousness does not abolish other, complementary differentiations and specializations, whether social, sexual, practical, aesthetic, scientific, philosophic, historical, or theological. Nor is this multiplicity in any way opposed to integration. For in each of such diverse patterns of conscious operation one is oneself in accord with some facet of one's being and some part of one's universe; and while one lives in only one pattern at a time in some cycle of recurrence, still the subject is over time, each pattern complements, reinforces, liberates the others, and there can develop a differentiation of consciousness to deal explicitly with differentiations of consciousness. That pattern is, of course, reflective subjectivity in philosophy and in theology. It follows the Hellenic precept "Know thyself." It follows the example of Augustinian recall, scrutiny, penetration, judgment, evaluation, decision. It realizes the modern concern for the authenticity of one's existing without amputating one's own rational objectivity expressed in propositional truth.

Fourthly, maturity understands the immature. It has been

through that, and it knows what it itself has been. It is aware that in childhood, before reaching the age of reason, one perforce works out one's quite pragmatic criteria for distinguishing between the "really real" and the merely imagined, desired, feared, dreamt, the sibling's trick, joke, fib. Still more clearly is it aware of the upset of crisis and conversion that is needed to purge oneself of one's childish realism and swing round completely and coherently to a critical realism. So it understands just how it is that some cling to a naive realism all their lives, that others move on to some type of idealism, that others feel some liberation from idealism in a phenomenology or an existentialism while, at the opposite extreme, there is a conceptualist extrinsicism for which concepts have neither dates nor developments and truth is so objective that it gets along without minds.

Such is the disorientation of contemporary experience, its inability to know itself and its own resources, the root of not a little of its insecurity and anxiety. Theology has to take this fact into consideration. The popular theology devised in the past for the *simplices fideles* has to be replaced. Nor will some single replacement do; for theology has to learn to speak in many modes and on many levels and even to minister to the needs of those afflicted with philosophic problems they are not likely to solve.

There remains, finally, the contention that "the ultimate epistemological consequence of the real distinction between essence and existence in creatures is to render the *intellect* incompetent for knowing the actual existence of *any* essence, be it created or uncreated, necessary or contingent" (p. 158). In this statement the emphasis seems to lie not on the reality of the distinction but on the mere existence of any, even a notional, distinction. For the author has just argued:

. . . the doctrine that there is in God *no real* distinction between essence and existence implies that nonetheless there is a *conceptual* distinction between them. We *cannot* empirically intuit the real indistinction of essence and existence in God. We *must* nonetheless conceive the two as distinct. There is, therefore, an unbridgeable difference between the way in which God is *in himself* and the way in which he is *in our knowledge*. Therefore, unless God were the object of empirical intuition, our concepts are *in principle* unable to make known to us the actual existence of God. For, as Kant was to conclude. . . . [p. 158]

Now this argument has a certain validity if in fact human knowing consists in concepts and empirical intuitions. But empirical intuition is just a misleading name for the givenness of the data of sense and of consciousness. In linking data to conception, there are inquiry and gradually developing understanding. The result of all these together is not knowledge but just thinking. To reach knowledge, to discern between astronomy and astrology, chemistry and alchemy, history and legend, philosophy and myth, there are needed the further activities of reflection, doubting, marshaling and weighing the evidence, and judging. Finally, this process of judging, in an important because clear instance, is like scientific verification, not as verification is imagined by the naïve to be a matter of looking, peering, intuiting, but as verification in fact is found to be, namely, a cumulative convergence of direct and indirect confirmations any one of which by itself settles just nothing.

I quite agree, then, that our concepts are in principle unable to make known to us the actual existence of God. I would add that they are in principle unable to make known to us the actual existence of anything. For concepts are just thinking; thinking is not knowing; it is only when we reach judgment that we attain human knowledge of anything whatever, whether of essence or existence, whether of creature or Creator.

There is, however, a further point; for Dewart asserts an unbridgeable difference between the way in which God is in Himself and the way in which He is in our knowledge. This, of course, while absolutely possible, is not possibly known within our knowledge, and so the reader may wonder how Dewart got it into his knowledge. The fallacy seems to be Dewart's confusion of thinking and knowing. In our thinking we may distinguish a concept of divine existence from a concept of divine essence. In our knowing we may affirm (1) that we think in the above manner and (2) that there is no distinction between the reality of the divine essence and the reality of the divine existence. The contrast is, then, not between God in Himself and God in our knowledge, but between God in our knowledge and God in our thinking. Nor is there anything unbridgeable about this contrast or difference; for the thinking and judging occur within one and the same mind, and the whole function of our judging may be described as determining how much of our thinking is correct.

But let me conclude. On the dust cover of *The Future of Belief* Harvey Cox is credited with the opinion: "A mature, highly erudite, and utterly radical book. It could be epoch-making." If for my part I have made certain reservations about the first two epithets, I must express the hope that the book will be epoch-making in the sense that it will contribute forcefully to the removal from theology of the many limitations of Hellenism. To that topic I shall in due time return.

8.

Dewart's View of Christian Philosophy and Contemporary Man

JOSEPH OWENS, C.SS.R.

LESLIE DEWART'S BOOK, *The Future of Belief,* moves within the theological arena. Nevertheless, it touches upon issues of crucial concern to Christian philosophy. From this viewpoint it prompts queries. Of these some are epistemological and metaphysical in character, others involve the historical development of Christian thought, while still others bear upon the attitude of the Christian philosopher toward a faith accepted solely upon divine authority, on the one hand, and toward theology on the other. Even though the views expressed in the book be considered as retailed from previously published works, their assemblage in popular and pleasantly written form seems to justify a few scrutinizing interrogations in the three areas just mentioned.

I

Fundamental in the epistemological area is the book's assertion that "no Christian believer today (unless he can abstract himself from contemporary experience) can understand *suppositum* or *hypostasis* as the primary subject of existence, action and attribution, but only as the primary object of consciousness" (p. 150). Epistemologically, this assertion implies a cleavage from traditional Scholastic thinking so primal and so radically conditioning everything else, that absolutely speaking the sole course indicated for a Scholastic is to register outright disagreement. Yet the context here allows room for a query. Upon whom does this *latae sententiae* excommunication fall? Does it not strike squarely upon the shoulders of every Christian believer who, in the Aristotelian tradition of Western philosophy, sees that human thought is directly of things and only concomitantly of itself? But does not Dewart's book presuppose throughout as its very *raison d'être* that there *still* are and will continue to be many such intransigent Christian believers *within* the fold, and that their influence has to be counteracted in crusading fashion? Indeed, one does not have to go beyond the epistemological writings of just two thinkers deeply immersed in contemporary experience and prominently mentioned in the book, Gilson and Maritain, to see that in point of fact there are still Christian believers in good standing who regard sensible composites as existent and as acting in independence of any human consciousness, and as knowable in that priority.

Is not this alone amply sufficient to excite both reservations concerning the book's notion of contemporary experience and wonder about the extent to which it is raising the telescope to the blind eye in its survey of the contemporary cosmos? The book assumes that "contemporary experience is an inhospitable environment for Christian belief" (p. 8) and that "it is the contemporary experience *as a whole* that is incongruous with Christian belief *as a whole*" (p. 17). If these statements have any importance, they must mean that in comparison with other epochs the present is incongruous with and inhospitable toward Christian belief. Yet if one compares the present world with preceding eras, can one uphold these assertions in any relevant sense? When in past epochs close enough for us to understand could a Catholic have been elected to the U.S. presidency, as in 1960, or a pope have been invited to address the world's nations, as in 1965? One would have to be stone deaf, it is true, to be unaware of dissatisfaction with traditional beliefs and practices on the part of many present-day Catholics—they shout it from the housetops. But does one not meet in daily life even more Catholics, not nearly so vocal, who experience no special incongruity in living a full modern life in the vivifying spirit of their faith? Some, in fact, are explicit in finding present-day conditions more congenial to the practice of their belief than any others in which they have lived or of which they have read. Does not the experience of these people, from leading intellectuals through a cross section of the Catholic world, form part of "contemporary experience"? Can it be excluded from "contemporary experience *as a whole*"?

Particularly disturbing, in this quite apparent refusal to meet contemporary experience in a realistic and integral way, is the book's attitude (pp. 28–29) toward the emphasis placed by popular preaching on reward and punishment. The emphasis is labeled a "spiritual hedonism which is above all concerned with the safety of one's immortal soul" (p. 74). *With Fontinell the book takes for granted that there is an incompatibility between eschatological motives and genuine love of God.* Yet the sturdily realistic gospels, as well as centuries of Christian tradition, stress eternal reward and punishment without feeling contradiction between the virtues of hope and charity. Does lived Christian experience feel any? Why should not one strive to gain heaven and avoid hell because that is what God wishes? In characteristically Christian teaching and experience the idealistic notion of virtue just for virtue's sake is conspicuously absent. Even the realistic Aristotelian motive of virtuous conduct for the sake of good (*kalon*) is not present. The motive, mirrored clearly in the Church's pastoral practice and teaching, is to serve a personal God. Thereby, with divine grace, one merits unending happiness after death, as opposed to everlasting frustration in hell. For Christian experience today, as through the centuries, there is no more clash between hope and charity than there was for St. Paul.

Finally, does not the approach from consciousness blur the starting point for the demonstration that God exists? True, one could judge that the consciousness exists and trace the existence to subsistent existence. But the approach does not lend itself to knowing existence through judgment. The directly known existence of sensible things in the external world and their reflexively known cognitional existence in one's mind, however, set off a clearly etched starting point for cogent reasoning to existence that subsists. In contrast to any ontological procedure from notion to existence, the existence is reached first and is then shown to be a nature and to coincide with the God of Christian belief. Is not the book prevented by its epistemological approach from seeing demonstrative cogency in this reasoning to God's existence? Not by chance, it acknowledges (p. 153), have the problems of existence of objects and existence of God been paralleled historically. That is faint praise. The reason is deeply metaphysical and independent of Parmenides.

II

The book calls for a *"dehellenization of dogma,* and specifically that of the Christian doctrine of God" (p. 49). But where was there hellenization, in any historical sense? Did not the Greek fathers, expressing Christian notions in forms of their own thought, successfully clear the concepts of anything opposed to creation, to divine omnipotence, to God's freedom in dealing with the world? And where in pre-Christian Greek philosophy do you find the *notions* of person, essence or subsistence? Even when Greek concepts such as substance, accident, word and nature were used, were they not painfully hammered into new shape to convey Christian content? Take a quick journey through pagan Greek philosophy and religion. Compare them with traditional Christian belief. Do you need anything more to apply here the observation of Galen that the doctrine of Moses differs from that of Plato and of all right thinking Greeks? Our intellectual debt to Greek thought is tremendous, but never did it hellenize Christian thought. Some Greek concepts, rather, were Christianized, and new ones were forged.

In dealing with the Scholastics the book becomes mildly amazing. It speaks of "the Scholastic theory of truth" (p. 86) and asserts: "In Scholastic philosophy God is not conceived as *a* being" (p. 173); "it is precisely as created *beings* that God's creatures must be totally contingent" (p. 154); *"as a reflexive analysis of our knowledge reveals,* there is in created being a real distinction between essence and existence" (p. 159); "to St. Thomas . . . the doctrine that God has no essence would have appeared absurd" (p. 183); "it was because he *was* a saint that one can be morally certain that St. Thomas did not practice what he preached" (p. 33). So frequent and so blatant are misunderstandings like these that the only feasible query in this area is to ask how many of the great Scholastics Dewart has seriously read.

The book observes that "the mainstream of Catholic *philosophy* has remained Scholastic" (p. 210). Will it not continue so? A survey of Canadian universities last year showed that Plato, Aristotle and Kant, in that order of incidence, were the leading formative influences in undergraduate philosophical instruction.

They, rather than analysts, phenomenologists or existentialists, will presumably be basic in coming Western philosophy. In this matrix, enlivened by strong Scholastic ferment, Christian philosophy should continue to thrive. In fact, recent escalation in the edition of necessary Scholastic texts, and the breakthrough in the art of reading the philosophy that Scholastic texts contain, promise a truly bright future for Scholastic philosophy in spite of so much current Catholic reaction against it.

III

On the attitude of Scholastics toward faith, the book alleges "circularity": "For God can be considered by us to be authoritative only if we *first* believe in God" (p. 71). Is not this in full accord with the book's denial (p. 206) of any operative distinction between the natural and the supernatural? The distinction "becomes a mere play on words, irrelevant to reality" (p. 210). A Christian philosopher, however, does not look for any rational generation of faith from philosophy. He recognizes as sufficient for the infusion of faith anything from a child's belief in the word of his parents to the hypothetical case of a metaphysician who had first demonstrated God's existence. If the decision is prudent, the conditions for divine faith are present. The Christian philosopher accepts the teaching of the Church on the basis of this faith, not on the basis of his philosophy. He will focus his philosophical scrutiny upon what he believes and elucidate it on the philosophical level. For instance, against the background of what he believes, his own study of human nature as endless can make him see how man is essentially incomplete. Here one faces a strange paradox. There was a time when Duns Scotus could note, in the prologue to his *Ordinatio,* that the philosophers regard nature as a finished whole while the theologians know it is defective. Now we have a theology denying completion by the supernatural while a Christian philosophy opens the way for its functioning.

Dewart remarks that "Catholic *theology* . . . has increasingly turned to non-Christian, secular thought for philosophical help" (p. 210; cf. p. 153). Theology and Christian philosophy have indeed been going, and may continue to go, entirely separate ways in dealing with the faith. Liaison between the American Catholic Philosophical Association and the American Catholic Theological Society, for example, has been practically non-existent. There are reasons. Certainly unacceptable, however, is the one alleged by Dewart that Scholasticism tends to "preclude *creative* development" (p. 153). Present-day Scholasticism is surely creative, not in the sense of spinning out grandiose systems, but in carefully developing what has already been begun, as in the case of the endlessness of man. At present and for years to come, Scholasticism will concentrate on recovering what the past has done. Yet even in doing this a Christian philosopher has to be creative, for never in the past has there been an authentic Scholastic philosophy developed as philosophy. Far from precluding creative development, genuine Scholastic philosophy cannot help but spark it.

Traditionally, Christian philosophy was regarded as the handmaid of theology. Suarez, setting aside his theological work to write the *Metaphysical Discussions,* illustrates how keenly the need of its services was felt. Today wealthy families get along without domestic help. Can theology do so, or afford to seek it elsewhere? It would be an impertinence for me to volunteer an answer, for I am not a theologian. But without a strong philosophical framework, can theology protect itself against the freewheeling that could turn it into a wonderland of nonsense? Scholastic thinking, of course, can give the framework. That theology turns to non-Christian thought for help is, however, its

99

own business. Yet on this point, on which I am incompetent to give an opinion, I feel in full accord with Dewart's observation: "One can only hope that this unfortunate state of affairs will not continue indefinitely" (p. 153).

The faith continues to be stated clearly in the official documents of Vatican Council II and the pronouncements of the Holy See. It is the same faith that we have known for centuries. But the effort necessary for a Christian philosopher to pursue his work *in spite of* much current theology is well illustrated in a remark made recently by the head of a philosophy department: "When I read so much of what is written today, I become depressed; then I take up a statement of the present Pope, regain my spirits and fervently thank God for Paul VI." This bifurcation, I agree, is bad. The pendulum, however, may start its return swing—let us hope not to an extreme—and some decades hence theology may look back a bit shamefacedly on its days of exuberant freewheeling after sudden release from Victorian and early twentieth-century straightjackets. In the meantime, patience, and—no matter how radically and outspokenly we disagree—in all things charity.

II.

1.

Orthodoxy Recast

GREGORY BAUM, O.S.A.

THE PROBLEM Leslie Dewart has chosen to treat is the integration of Christian faith with the everyday experience of contemporary man. Dewart feels that the sphere of religion expressed in traditional terms appears as an artificial world, a sort of foreign body within the context of contemporary intellectual experience. Even the believer, Dewart thinks, tends to regard his belief in God as an insertion into the continuity of his life from without. What are the reasons for this estrangement?

The title of Dewart's book recalls Freud's study on religion, *The Future of an Illusion.* Could Freud have been correct in regarding religion as a projection of wish-fulfillment? Will the education for reality, which Freud sought to foster and which modern civilization promotes, eventually wean men from religion altogether? Professor Dewart thinks not. He agrees with Freud that religion as wish-fulfillment is a widely spread phenomenon. But since Dewart is firmly convinced that the self-revealing God proclaimed in the Gospel is at the center of human existence, he blames the circumstance that belief in God is almost unassimilable to modern life on the inability of the Church to speak of the divine mystery except in terms taken from a culture that has disappeared. Dewart insists that the

Church must find a new conceptualization of the Gospel, a conceptualization that corresponds to contemporary intellectual experience.

The insistence on the radical reform of dogma puts Dewart in the company of Protestant and Anglican authors, such as Bultmann, Tillich and Bishop Robinson, who have attempted to reformulate the Christian faith in modern terms. Dewart agrees with these authors that religion does not intend to say anything about a special sphere of life separated from this world, about an elevated or supernatural reality somewhere else, but speaks of that which happens at the center of human life, of man's progress in self-knowledge, of his growing sensitivity to the real, of his entry into full responsibility for himself and his environment. Dewart agrees with these authors that it is the fault of religious people and their religious language that it is so difficult to communicate the fact that belief in God does not affirm his presence in a distant world but his presence in this world.

What is peculiar to Professor Dewart—and herein lies the significance of his work—is that he develops his radical theology as a committed Roman Catholic who accepts the divine revelation in Jesus Christ as preached by the Church throughout the centuries. Dewart holds that the Catholic Church has always been faithful to the essential core of the revealed Gospel. What Dewart denies is that the Church's fidelity to divine revelation, in technical terms "her infallibility," logically implies immutability of dogma. Dewart provides a theory of truth which enables him to affirm that the Church has always been faithful to divine revelation and at the same time to demand a radical reinterpretation of doctrine.

The core of Dewart's book (Chapter 3) is philosophical. He contrasts the classical understanding of truth (conformity of the mind to an object extrinsic to it) with an understanding of truth, more in line with contemporary phenomenology, as the fidelity of consciousness to its own expansive vitality. Dewart refuses to follow classical philosophy in regarding knowledge as the union of the knower (subject) and the known (object) in the knower; knowledge cannot be explained on the basis of an original dichotomy between subject and object, for the simple reason that the differentiation between subject and object, or self and non-self, is already knowledge. Initially man encounters his own undifferentiated relations to his environment, and it is precisely through a process of self-differentiation, that he is able to know non-self as distinct from himself, and through this very process become present to himself or achieve consciousness.

Dewart distinguishes between experience and consciousness. While man's experience of reality is never separated from consciousness, or conceptualization, by which this experience becomes present to him and communicable, the same experience could be conceptualized in different ways. Human experience does not necessitate any particular form of conceptualization. Dewart follows Wittgenstein in affirming that this process of conceptualization is socio-historical. It would be incorrect to say that man's experience has an inner reality for him which he, then, tries to express in concepts and words: what is true, rather, is that man becomes conscious of his experience through the conceptualization to which his society introduces him. Conceptualization of experience is not a perfection added to man's being; it is rather constitutive of man as a self-conscious person.

Dewart then defines truth in terms of consciousness. Through consciousness the self differentiates itself out of the totality of continuous reality, and the growing development of the self takes place to the extent that the world is conceptualized, systemized, lived with and made meaningful for consciousness. Truth is the quality of the intellectual life that seeks to heighten consciousness. Truth is "not the result of the mind's 'inner' reduplicative, intentional reflection of an object 'outside' it," truth is rather "the

105

result of the mind's coming-into-being through the self-differentiation of that-which-is into self and world" (p. 93). Truth is attained through the intensification of consciousness.

The distinction between "experience" and "consciousness," inseparable though they be, is applied by Dewart to the Church's faith in divine revelation. In keeping with contemporary theological understanding, Dewart does not regard divine revelation as a message once made known to us through Jesus Christ; divine revelation is the definitive self-communication of God in Jesus Christ, identically continued in the Church and constitutive of her being. The Church's acknowledgment of this revelation in faith is what Dewart would call her "experience"—which does not exist in her except in a particular conceptualization or form of consciousness. In keeping with his own theory, Dewart insists that the conceptualization of the Church's response to revelation is a socio-historical process. The Church's faith in God revealing is made present to herself and to others through a conceptualization which she receives, actively and creatively, from the culture to which she belongs. And since truth can only be preserved if man seeks to intensify his consciousness, the Church cannot preserve the Gospel by clinging to a conceptualization of the past, in particular to the hellenic form of Christian consciousness; the Church must conceptualize her response to divine revelation in a form taken from contemporary intellectual culture which, according to Dewart, embodies a greater self-consciousness of man or a greater presence of man to himself.

Dewart proposes a program of radical dehellenization of Christian faith—while giving a positive meaning to the Catholic teaching on the continuity and infallibility of the Church. Whether his attempt will be successful in the Catholic Church will depend on whether, in dialogue with other theologians, he will be able to specify the criteria of orthodoxy that must guide the re-conceptualization of Christian faith. Are there norms by which the Church can test whether she has been faithful in her quest for heightened consciousness?

Dewart applied his method of dehellenization to the reality beyond being but present to being which we call God (Chapters 5 and 6).

The contemporary expression of Christian faith, however tentative it may be, enables Dewart to engage in fruitful dialogue with humanists and atheists. Of special significance is his chapter on contemporary atheism and Christian theism (Chapter 2). He tries to show that contemporary Marxists are "relative atheists." By this he means that they are opposed to God, not on the basis of some absolute principle, but rather because they regard religion as a conservative or anti-revolutionary force in society. If a reconceptualization of the Christian Gospel were to make believers more sensitive to social problems and the need to transform society, i.e., if Christianity became a revolutionary movement, these Marxists would not persevere in their unqualified rejection of religion. They would be able to cooperate with religion in changing society. Conversely, Professor Dewart tries to show that Christians are not "absolute theists" but "relative theists." For a Christian the affirmation of God is not an ultimate. He subjects every affirmation of God to a critical analysis and accepts it as a statement about God only if it fulfills certain criteria given in the Gospel. An "absolute theist" would ally himself with anyone or any party who affirms God's existence in his world view or program of action. The Christian, Dewart says, critically examines which God there is question of. Since the Bible says, "He who does not love does not know God," the Christian realizes that a person, or a party, who affirms God in the Christian creed may in fact not be talking about the true God at all. If, to follow one criterion of the New Testament, this person or party does not love, i.e., if he is not involved in human life in a special way, then he is not speaking of the true God at all. He does not know the true God. The Christian is a "relative theist" because his critique of statements about God might bring him into closer association with men who deny God's existence than with those who, in a particular social and political context, affirm it. It is possible, Dewart concludes, that Marxists as "relative atheists" and Christians as "relative theists" may, under conditions that always remain in need of critical examination, be involved in fruitful dialogue and cooperation in building society.

The publication of *The Future of Belief* is an important event in the history of theological literature on the North American continent. No theologian, no Catholic theologian at least, will be able to overlook Dewart's work. It is not difficult to understand why the book is provoking rather vehement opposition in some theological circles. Dewart seriously challenges the philosophical thinking traditional in the Church and at times manifests undisguised hostility to the intellectual achievements of the past—even though his own theory of knowledge would have enabled him to be more appreciative of systems of thought which he regards as outmoded. The book, moreover, raises many problems for which no answers are immediately available. The problems will have to be thought and lived through by the theological community and only time will tell whether the door that was opened leads to a promising future of belief.

2.

The Need for Radicalism

EUGENE FONTINELL

THE FUTURE OF BELIEF will be the most discussed, debated, praised and denounced philosophical work within the Roman Catholic community for some time to come. No book since Teilhard's *The Phenomenon of Man* has so seriously threatened the conventions of Roman Catholic thought. Despite its intellectual depth and occasional technical complexity, however, this work is addressed not to professional philosophers but to reflective men in general and reflective Roman Catholics in particular.

The comparison to Teilhard is suggestive. For one thing, Dewart maintains the thrust of Teilhard's vision while placing it within a much more sophisticated philosophical and theological framework. For another, it will be impossible to do with Dewart what has been done with Teilhard: to denounce him initially and then, when he refuses to go away, to claim that he is easily assimilable within traditional Catholic categories. The old three-stage approach—"it's false"; "it may be true but it's dangerous"; "well of course we had it all the time"—will not work with Dewart's thought. He has command of and respect for the philosophical underpinnings of Catholic life but convincingly demonstrates that these underpinnings cannot assimilate contemporary thought and experience.

Because it cannot be assimilated, *The Future of Belief* is likely to split the Roman Catholic community; or, more accurately, to bring to the surface a split that is already there.

Let me put the matter bluntly: an increasing number of Catholic philosophers find that the traditional hellenic metaphysics, which has shaped the Western and Christian mind, is no longer a viable philosophical worldview. So long as such a philosopher ignores theological tradition he will provoke debate but not division. But, and Dewart is not the only man engaged in the enterprise, as soon as he applies his contemporary worldview to the conventional categories of Catholic theology, he is forced to the admission that those categories are incompatible with this worldview—they stifle thinking and retard experience. Such a philosopher may keep quiet, or he may express his thought only in technical journals. Or he may, as Dewart has done, attempt to rethink his faith in terms of a contemporary worldview and publish the results in a language and style that communicate to a wide audience.

Since Dewart has made the latter choice, he is bound to provoke division, and a painful division at that. The pain would be less were it possible for him to prove Hellenism wrong and his own processive metaphysics right. However great my agreement with Dewart, I do not think his arguments are susceptible of proof (any more than are arguments in favor of the Greek worldview). As a result I can only urge the reader to take seriously the *possibility* that Dewart's direction may in fact be the future of belief; just as Dewart admits the possibility that he may be wrong. On the one hand he maintains that both his orientation and the traditional one "seem to be perfectly possible within the strictest orthodoxy." On the other, he stresses the radical nature of his vision and even admits that "the conservatives may have been closer to the mark when they have 'alerted' the Church to a profound division within the Catholic faith" than were those liberals who glossed over all splits. These same conservatives, he later says, are possibly right when they insist "that the Church's decision to recognize the reality of freedom and conscience can only result in the eventual disappearance of Christianity in the form in which we have known it since primitive times."

The seriousness of the division between traditional and contemporary metaphysics is great. Both viewpoints can, I hope, co-exist for a time, but only one will, I believe with Dewart, survive. It is urgent that, during the period of co-existence, we recognize that the only valid criterion of any theory of truth, of any dogma or expression of Christianity (and all expressions are to some extent theories), is the quality of life to which it gives rise. Dewart expresses this when he says that "Christianity has a *mission,* not a *message.*" Further, that what the Church communicates as the "historical vehicle of God's self-communication to man . . . is its reality and existence, not an idea."

The question which so starkly confronts Catholics is, can we continue to live, act, talk and pray together while disagreeing profoundly? One should not too glibly respond "Oh yes!" for it is by no means certain that we can and it is most certain that at best it will not be easy. Our fundamental theories and ideas, in so far as they are vital, must continually form us and thus, to the extent that they differ, they threaten our "community"—that which we have in common. The effort to achieve a unity that includes radical differences will be a most severe test for the Roman Catholic Church but it is perhaps not a purely parochial undertaking; it might be seen as a paradigm for any future unity of Christians and finally of all men.

Throughout *The Future of Belief* Dewart maintains a tone and level of discourse conducive to disagreement without denunciation. He makes clear that he is merely sketching his "proposal in broad outline, in order to try it on the touchstone of public elimination." Though his criticism of Catholicism is one of the most severe criticisms ever made by a believing Catholic, it is singularly free from any hint of the neurosis and fanaticism that can permeate such efforts. At the same time he completely avoids playing that game, which has taken the energy of so many brilliant contemporary Catholic thinkers, of having to write in such fashion that they appear not to say what they are really saying. For the most part, Dewart expresses in clear and unequivocal language the serious implications of bringing the Church abreast of contemporary thought and experience.

Take, for example, the chapter on "The Development of Christian Dogma," in many ways the most significant and crucial chapter in the book. It would be hard to find any Catholic today who is against the "development of Christian dogma," but it will be quite easy to find many Catholics who will reject Dewart's view of the issue.

The reason is simply that Dewart explicitly denies that theory of development which is the refuge of even the best of the Catholic thinkers who are trying to come to terms with a processive world. I refer to the classical view that dogma or truth change accidentally while remaining substantially or essentially the same. Dewart maintains that such a distinction must be held only if one insists on remaining within hellenic patterns of thought. He insists that Christian theism has a future, however, only on the condition that it jettison the hellenic concepts and categories which it has acquired and begin to forge new concepts more congenial to contemporary experience.

The necessity for such an undertaking is not a superficial need to be *au courant* or to achieve better public relations with the world. The necessity stems rather from the fact that reflective men no longer do or can live within hellenic categories. A theism, therefore, which insists on remaining within those categories is assuring itself of death or, what amounts to the same thing, human irrelevancy.

Contemporary man is characterized by his awareness of himself as a socio-historical being and Dewart's contention is that such awareness is consistent with an authentic Christian theism. This means, however, that all concepts, including our concept of God, are conditioned sociologically, culturally and historically. The believer need not lament this situation, particularly if he bears in mind that "belief must bear *directly* upon the reality of God, not upon words or upon concepts." Dewart is not suggesting here some kind of "mystical, immanentist, or other extraordinary cognitive union," for all faith involves concepts. It is important to note, however, that in Dewart's theory of knowledge concepts are participational rather than representational. Concepts do not *re*-present or stand-for objects existing "out there;" rather, they are means for participation in and development of human life. In Dewart's words, "Conceptualization is the socio-historical process by which consciousness, and man as such, evolve." As for the conceptualization of faith, it "is a process by which we render ourselves *present* to that-in-which-we-believe." Thus Dewart is able to advance an interpretation of faith which combines both an existential personalism and a philosophy of process.

On Dewart's terms the development of doctrine is something not to be tolerated but celebrated: it is a sign of life. A theism that excluded the possibility of development, which did not indeed demand development, would "be a facile and indiscriminate theism which cares more for belief than for the reality, God, to which belief should be merely a way." Christian faith, on the other hand, "is *both* belief and dis-belief" and prohibits the believer from ever resting content with the belief of the moment. "It is this need for critical discrimination that makes the Christian faith essentially unstable, searching and dependent upon constant renewal and development."

It is in the last chapter of *The Future of Belief,* when Dewart

113

raises the question as to how Christianity is "likely to reconceptualize consciously its belief in God," that many readers will part company with him. Dewart goes out of his way "to stress the tentative and exploratory character" of his remarks. Further, he has in an earlier chapter, when dealing with the traditional theistic concepts which have been borrowed from the Greeks, conceded that "we have not to date managed to do better." He goes on to say, however, that "it is because we *have not* managed to do better that we must *depart* therefrom and proceed forth." And depart Dewart does. He suggests that "the Christian theism of the future might not conceive God as *a being;*" "and if he is not a being he does not exist." God as person, omnipotent, eternal and supernatural, all of these concepts including even the name "God" may some day be judged inappropriate for a theism "come of age."

A final note. Dewart's work is addressed primarily to Roman Catholics and will be upsetting primarily to them, but its implications are not restricted to this particular community. We have here a splendid example of a man having the courage to question even his most cherished assumptions. It has been my experience that very few men are able to maintain a sustained criticism of their own assumptions. Even those theoretically most critical of absolutes usually protect a few assumptions from the merciless eye of reflective criticism. That a thinker such as Dewart can emerge out of and choose to remain within a community that has become almost identified with absolutism and immutability, surely must pose a challenge to the hidden absolutes of all men— whether Christian, atheist, or humanist. Some years ago a critic of the Roman Catholic's effort to be really open-minded when it came to religious questions charged that the Catholic thinker "performs his acrobatics over a net." However one may finally evaluate Dewart's "acrobatics," no one can deny that he has dared to remove the net.

3.

An Ecumenical
Convergence

HARVEY COX

> In my opinion, the world will not be converted to the heavenly
> promises of Christianity unless Christianity has previously been con-
> verted . . . to the promises of earth.—*Pierre Teilhard de Chardin.*

IT IS CERTAINLY TIME to bring to a close the decades-long war
of attrition between Christianity and communism. Nothing more
exacerbates the global confrontation between East and West than
the rhetoric that bills it as a duel to the death between God and
atheism. Nothing so adds lethal danger to the Vietnam war as
the twisted misconstruction of it into an Armageddon between
the knights of Christian civilization and the dragons of godless-
ness. Propagandists of the church and of the various communist
parties have stoked the fires of frenzy without ceasing. One
reason why Americans find it so difficult to think rationally about
world revolution is that they have been fed so long on the
strident anticommunism of the American churches. Who could
count the communion-breakfast speeches, sermons and pastoral
admonitions that have drummed up the image of a world strug-

gle between the hosts of God and the hosts of Satan? Or—a more subtle form of the same propaganda—the number of times we have been asked to support Christian missions, rally behind foreign aid, contribute to Radio Free Europe, even defend land reform, because if we did not those whom we denied our concern would certainly become Reds? As though a Christian—or any sensitive human being—needed this kind of threat to induce him to help make food, clothing or truthful information available to his neighbor.

Either religion in one of its forms or Marxism in one of its varieties is now the controlling life view for most of the world's people. At the same time thermonuclear weapons have made the Thermopylae interpretation of this state of affairs infinitely dangerous. Is there any possibility that in the last third of our war-weary 20th century the two protagonists in this deadly, dagger-drawn duel can begin to work out a way of living together?

Two books issued simultaneously this fall suggest that we may at last be on the threshold of a new era in communist-Christian relationships. For the past two years a group of (mainly Catholic) German-speaking Christians called the Paulus Society have been meeting with a group of European Marxist intellectuals. One of the most articulate of these Marxists is the Frenchman Roger Garaudy. Out of his experience in the developing conversation Garaudy has written a short book tracing the changed attitude of Catholics and communists alike to the fact that they inhabit the same planet. The American Catholic publishing firm of Herder and Herder had the book translated from the original French and issued it under the title *From Anathema to Dialogue*. This was an unprecedented move, since Herder had never before published a book by a communist. Therefore the firm asked Leslie Dewart, a Catholic who is professor of philosophy at St. Michael's College of the University of Toronto, to write an

116

answer to Garaudy. Professor Dewart agreed, the more readily because his earlier book, *Christianity and Revolution,* covered some of the same ground. Hence these two volumes, both of them milestones in American religious thought—Garaudy's because it exposes Americans to an intelligent and sympathetic Marxist critique of religion rather than to the inane testimony of cosmonauts who reported that they had not seen any angels; Dewart's because it takes the Marxist critique with the utter seriousness it deserves and then moves on to the first stages of a risky but enormously imaginative reconstruction of the doctrine of God.

I

Even without Dewart's, Garaudy's book could hardly fail to make a mark on the American religious scene; and even without Garaudy's, Dewart's book would be a major new achievement in the English-speaking theological world. Together they provide more than enough thrust to lift theological discussion to a new level of interest and clarity.

Like any Marxist, Mr. Garaudy believes that the emerging dialogue is possible only because of today's changed social and political conditions. Among these are the one-third of the world which is now in some way communist, the rapid expansion of science and technology, and the throwing off of colonial rule in Africa and Asia. (He might have cited two other events sometimes classified by insurance companies as "acts of God," namely the death of Stalin and of Pope Pius XII.) But Garaudy also emphasizes intellectual currents. He mentions the favorable theological atmosphere induced by Barth's movement from *The Epistle to the Romans* to *The Humanity of God,* by the efforts of Bultmann and his followers to distinguish between the real gospel and dated, prescientific world views, and by the impact of Bishop John Robinson's *Honest to God.* All this, he says, has led both Christians and Marxists to a new appreciation of "what is basic" and what is not in their respective points of view.

It is not surprising that in his chapter on the Christian rediscovery of what is basic Garaudy makes large use of Teilhard de Chardin. He praises Teilhard not only for his attempts to save Christianity from its doltish opposition to science but for his insistence that no man can be saved "except through an extension of the universe," as the Jesuit paleontologist once said. Garaudy also agrees with Teilhard's dissent from the usual interpretation of the doctrine of original sin—an interpretation Teilhard called "the tight collar which strangles our minds and hearts." Garaudy is not the only Marxist with a soft spot for this Roman priest. He is admired especially among the young and orthodox European Marxist intellectuals.

Garaudy puts considerable stress on the contrast now being made between the "Constantinian tradition" in Christianity (close connection with the ruling classes, assimilation of Greco-Latin ideologies and their hierarchical conception of the world) and the "apocalyptic tradition" of primitive Christianity. The latter, as Garaudy sees it, reflects the period when Christianity was "a slave religion, . . . a protest, however weak, against the established order, and a hope for the coming of the Kingdom on earth as in heaven." In fact Garaudy, following (perhaps unconsciously) an old tradition in left-wing Christianity, has a theory of the "fall" of the church. Luther held that the fall of the church occurred in the fifth century, with the development of centralized papal authority. Garaudy pushes the fall further back (as did Münzer and Hus), into the fourth century, when Christianity became "an ideology of imperial justification and resignation."

But in Garaudy's opinion the fall did not finish off Christianity. This Marxist seems delighted at what he takes to be the

118

rebirth in our time of that apocalyptic tradition. He cites with enthusiasm the Jesuit Karl Rahner's characterization of Christianity (at the May 1965 Salzburg Christian-Marxist colloquy) as "the religion of the absolute future." And Garaudy obviously relishes today's rebirth of interest in the eschatological aspect of theology. In this connection he mentions the brilliant young Roman Catholic theologian Johannes Metz. He might also have mentioned such Protestants as Jürgen Moltmann and Gerhard Sauter.

II

It is clear that a dialogue between Christianity and Marxism is now possible. Both are talking about the full development of man (humanization and hominization). Both are concerned (each in its own time) with subjectivity and transcendence. Both are fascinated with the future and what it means for man's freedom, maturation and responsibility. But, as Garaudy realizes, the question now becomes: Is a dialogue *desirable?*

From the Marxist side, he says, the answer is an unequivocal Yes. Marxists seek to incorporate into their thinking all that is humanly valuable, wherever and however it has arisen. Garaudy is especially attentive to the epochal contribution Christianity made to civilization when it defined man as a free agent in time. He finds it hard to hide his enthusiasm for this part of the Christian theological tradition. He says:

With Christianity, a new status for man in regard to the world appeared, one which constituted a radical departure from that of Greek humanism. Existence, for man, is no longer a matter of being inserted into the Whole of the cosmos as one of its fragments. For man to exist has now become the liberation from his nature and his past, by the divine grace revealed in Christ, liberation for a life which consists in free decisions. As of this moment, authentic "history" has become possible: to the timeless contemplation of the eternal laws of the cosmos, there succeeds an unfolding of life in time, where the past is the *locus* of sin, where the future which lies always before us is the *locus* of grace, and where the present is the time for decision, the time for acceptance or rejection of the divine call.

I quote this section at length because it sums up better than many Christian theologians could the unique thrust of biblical faith: setting man as a responsible agent in history before an open future. Far from being a sacralization of the present or a canonization of the past, Christianity requires us to understand everything in the world in terms of the future, on the basis of what it could become if its potential were fully unlocked.

So dialogue is both possible and desirable for Marxists, at least for Garaudy. Unfortunately Garaudy cannot speak for Marshal Lin Piao and the Chinese Red Guards, nor even for the East European communist establishment. That many East European communists were denied visas for the Salzburg meeting indicates that in the minds of party hierarchs there remain considerable reservations about dialogue with Christians. Garaudy does not specifically mention this aspect of the problem, but he does concede that some Christians may find the frequent administrative harassment and occasional persecution of Christians and churches in communist countries an obstacle to honest encounter. These abuses he attributes to the narrow, rigid Marxist view of religion still held by many communists—a view he himself has often criticized openly. He is especially hard on communists who say they are ready to talk with Catholic workers, but "as workers, not as Catholics."

Yet this will not quite do. Possibly the horror stories in the right-wing Catholic and Protestant press about the persecution of Christians "behind the iron curtain" are somewhat exaggerated.

Nonetheless it is true that, especially in the U.S.S.R., pressuring the seminaries and legal pestering and closing of churches seem far from abating. One could of course point out that in Indonesia's recent anti-communist coup 400,000 persons suspected of being communists or having communist leanings were murdered. If that many Christians had been killed, by communists or anyone else anywhere in the world, we should never hear the end of it. As it was, there were but a few ripples of protest. Now everything seems to be forgotten, and we are rejoicing that Indonesia has "turned back from communism."

Still, countering accusations with accusations will never work. Garaudy is right in saying that Christians must decide whether they really want dialogue with communists, that no one else can make this decision for them. If they want dialogue they will have to accept certain preconditions. The first—which must be rigorously observed by both sides—is that one does not seek to destroy the dialogue partner. Garaudy holds that Marxism has now reached a stage where it not only can but must converse with Christianity. He knows that the problem of the person, of what he calls "subjectivity," is central for the next phase of Marxist theoretical development. He believes that in rejecting all of Christianity, Marxists have been insufficiently dialectical since Christianity is "right in the questions it raises about man and history" and wrong only in the answer it gives. Marxism, however, has not even begun to raise these questions. It must raise them now, and so dialogue is needed.

III

In no sense a rebuttal of Garaudy's, Professor Dewart's book is an attempt to respond to the Marxist critique of religion and of other elements that engage modern sensibility by undertaking a further constructive development of Christian theism. Thus it is a book about God and the doctrine of God—happily so; for not only does this approach meet the Marxist challenge precisely where it must be met, but it brings a powerful new contribution to bear in a theological situation still reeling from the recent "death of God" foray. It is perhaps unfortunate that Dewart has subtitled his book "Theism in a World Come of Age." True, he is trying to purify and sharpen for modern minds the concept of what it means to believe in God. But his solution goes so far beyond any previous types of theism that this subtitle may mislead. In his *The Courage to Be* (the 1954 Terry lectures), Paul Tillich talked about a God "beyond theism." But in comparison with Dewart's, Tillich's ideas seem cautious. It is Dewart's God rather than Tillich's who is "beyond theism."

In Dewart's very first chapter, "Christian Theism and Contemporary Experience," the reader becomes aware that he is in for a new departure in theological writing. The author insists that the everyday experience of twentieth-century men can no longer be simply discounted by theology, or attributed to error or cultural backsliding. Christians and non-Christians alike, he says, we are all part of the contemporary experience; hence it will not do to define the issue as merely "communicating" some sort of Christian idea to those outside. The church communicates itself; its task is to integrate itself with the modern world, not to sell it a product. The real issue is the self-evident conflict between faith and the *prima facie* experience of today's secular world.

IV

In attacking this problem Dewart makes grateful use of the critics who have uncovered the sources of the religious illusion, especially Freud and Marx. His citation of these two men is crucial not only because they present the most potent critique of religion but because both view religion in the context of personal or social development. Freud does not blame man for having religious illusions; he merely doubts that these illusions will endure now that science has come to the center of the stage. On his part, Marx refused to join the intellectual atheists of his day in trumpeting their version of death-of-God thinking. Except for a brief period early in his career, he had little interest in theism or atheism as such. He realized that religious systems spring from particular types of socio-economic structure and that theism would disappear when the social conditions that fostered it had been abolished, not in the face of verbal tirades. "The philosophers have interpreted the world in various ways," he said in his *Theses on Feuerbach,* "but the thing to do now is to change it."

Dewart likewise concedes that a certain form of theism might have been necessary and, given its historical setting, even healthy. But just as infants grow up and discard their childish fantasies, so societies require, and develop, conscious changes in their symbolizations. Dewart does not fault the church for the various doctrines of God it has elaborated in order to live in different historical periods. But he does insist that the development must now go further, that "Christian belief in its traditional form is at its most basic level not attuned to the contemporary experience of man. . . ."

What can be done? Dewart proposes a doctrine of God which moves completely beyond the classical epistemologies and metaphysics out of which our Christian concept of deity grew. He refuses to become enmeshed in a dispute about whether God "exists," since he considers mistaken the very notion of "existence" or even of "being" as prerequisite to reality. To exalt being as the ultimate category of reality not only traps us in static categories of thought but inevitably produces a political ethic which cannot make room for radical change. Thus Dewart—

obviously a master of Scholastic thought—also shows that he has understood the main point of the Marxist critique. He knows that doctrines of God reflect the social structure of given historical periods, but that after they have been elaborated they can retard social change by sacralizing the structures of the period in which they emerged. This circumstance explains why some type of atheism is always necessary for social change. It also explains why the atheist who takes himself too seriously reveals his own mental enmeshment in the same outdated period. Thus neither theism nor atheism can be "absolute." When either becomes absolute it denies the irreducibly historical character of any religious or antireligious belief. Both theism and atheism need to be aware of their conditional character and of their need to develop and change if they are to escape the rigidity of dogmatism.

Marxist atheism, unlike "death of God" atheism, is conditional, not absolute. It does not object to the doctrine of God abstractly or to any and every doctrine of God in general. It expressly denies the Christian doctrine of God as this doctrine has emerged and developed in history. And it objects to this doctrine not because of some esoteric vision of God's demise or because the notion seems empty to many people, but *because of what the Christian belief in God has done to inhibit man's maturation and to thwart social change.* Responding to Marxist atheism is thus a totally different thing from responding to "death of God" atheism. There is no conceivable doctrine or idea of God that could satisfy those who seriously believe in the "death" of God. Death is final. This is what makes their position ahistorical and incapable of development. For Marxist atheism, on the other hand, a doctrine of God that met their specific objections would at least move the conversation further along. Dewart does us all a momentous service by showing that it is atheism of the Marxist type, not of the death-of-God type, which is the real challenge to theology today.

Because it is conditional atheism that must be answered by a further development of theism, Dewart insists on our leaving firmly behind the unconditional theism of historical Christianity. We must energetically "dehellenize" Christian theology. This step calls for jettisoning the entire metaphysical framework in which our idea of God is housed. Here, Dewart in fact believes, Marxists have not gone far enough, have not been critical enough of their roots in Hegel and in idealism. Marxism "is not radical enough," he declares. "It is not enough to overcome idealism. It is also necessary to overcome metaphysics as a speculative ideology."

V

Dewart's final chapter, "The Development of Christian Theism," sketches an idea of God that does "overcome metaphysics as a speculative ideology." The author "overcomes metaphysics" by allowing himself to imagine how the doctrine of God might develop if it were reconstructed to meet the needs of our actual experience, not of metaphysical coherence. Such reconstruction could, for example, leave behind the "preoccupation with God's existence which characterized post-patristic thought, and hence post-medieval philosophy," and go on to work out what the fact of our *experience* of transcendence means. Dewart believes that in the process we could stop worrying about whether God exists or is a being, because we do not have to identify intelligibility with being. In other words, it is not necessary that something exist in order to have reality; it is only our hellenic bias that makes us think so. The future, for example, does not "exist" and has no "being" in any sense; nevertheless it is a reality in human experience.

What about God's "personality"? Dewart holds that this idiom must also be left behind in the next stage of Christian theism. The modern idea of personality restricts the reality of God and makes some form of atheism necessary. In a brief but enticing passage Dewart speculates on a view of God that could go beyond personal metaphors: "The typical experience of the disaffiliated religious person today is that 'God could not possibly be a person. He must be some kind of cosmic force.'" A naïve view, Dewart concedes. But he also thinks that it may express a correct hunch that God, rather than a center of being, is "an expansive force which impels persons to go out and beyond themselves." He even suggests that this naïve notion represents a legitimate indictment of one aspect of absolute theism, and that even so crude an insight "may yet be redeemed in the future of Christian theism."

No doubt this author's contribution to our understanding of God will anger and bewilder many Christians. It makes use of the Catholic assertion that doctrine "develops"—a venerable principle that served both Cardinal Newman and Karl Adam, though those gentlemen hardly foresaw what Dewart would do with it. Dewart employs the category of development not to justify what happened between a doctrine's beginnings and its present form, but to show what *could* happen to the present form, to make it viable in the future. How for example might the traditional idea of God's "omnipotence" be transcended? By letting "omnipotence" mean what it must, Dewart says; namely, that the world is totally open to God and therefore "totally open to *future creation by man.*" . . . "The case," he adds, "is not that God can do the impossible . . . but that for God all things are possible—and that therefore with God all things are possible to man." Thus the static idea of God's omnipotence would be transformed into a belief in "the radical openness of history—an openness which not even man's freedom can annihilate." The ethical consequence of this belief is twofold: we could no longer fall back on the superstitious notion of divine omnipotence, and we would have to take adult responsibility for the world. We would know, Dewart says, that unless we make it, "the Kingdom of God [will] never come."

This transformation of the idea of God's omnipotence demonstrates what startling possibilities open up if we recognize the need to develop further our present doctrines. It also joins the issue with the Marxists, in superb fashion. The Marxists' main objection to Christian theism is that it inhibits man from assuming complete control of the future. Engels, for example, says in his *Anti-Dühring* that "men themselves make history, only they do so in a given environment which conditions it, and on the basis of actual relations already existing." This famous sentence reveals one of Marxism's unresolved quandaries. Does man *really* make history and is the future *unconditionally* open? Or is there in history some "inner logic" to which man must ultimately conform if he is to be "free"? Marxism remains unclear on this point. At times Karl Marx's thinking seems to be influenced by a Hebrew view of the future as something utterly subject to man's free moral action; at other times his links with the Stoics and more particularly with Hegel conspire to reduce man's freedom to a kind of acquiescence in the inevitable dialectic.

VI

A viable Christian doctrine of God today must make man *more* responsible for history than Marxism does. In fact this, to my mind, is the final test of the adequacy of the doctrine for our time. Christianity—to quote Rahner again—"is the religion of the absolute future." Therefore it must break all its ties with teleology, with any belief in a fixed plan being worked out in history; and must recast its idioms of transcendence in such a way

127

that transcendence is seen as that unconditionally open future which elicits man's unreserved freedom in shaping his own future. Obviously the test of such a doctrine's validity could not be theoretical; it would have to be operational. Whether—or that—God is real is decided not by argumentation but by action in mission, by politics.

This new frame of reference for theology begins to shape up in Dewart's book. History itself now provides the inclusive horizon for theological thought. Thus Dewart rejects those notions of the incarnation which think of God as coming into terrestrial history on a sort of slumming jaunt. God, he insists, has taken up permanent residence in history, indeed becomes the very substance of history. The last supratemporal and extraterrestrial residue of Greek metaphysics is rinsed away and we find a God who is totally "with us" in the human enterprise. Thus Dewart represents a thoroughgoing incarnationalism, rather than the quasi-docetic incarnationalism that has plagued theology for so long. God is that presence within history which is not a part of history but makes history possible. This concept links Dewart to the recent school of eschatological theologians in Europe—such people as Gerhard Sauter, Johannes Metz, Jürgen Moltmann. These theologians also see God as the pressure for maturity and responsibility exerted on man by an unequivocally open future. If the word "God" has become too freighted with metaphysical overtones, Dewart is ready to accept a new word to designate this reality. "Wise people," he says, "do not worry about names."

The Future of Belief is not easy reading. By a process of careful and qualified reasoning it arrives at astonishing conclusions. Dewart does not simply toss out his spectacular assertions; he constructs them with meticulous respect for clarity of argument. But his cautious style of writing makes his ideas even more breathtaking. He avoids side issues and plunges into the very heart of the matter, the question on which our faith lives or dies:

the reality of the living God. In my opinion, we either move along the road Dewart has staked out or else we abandon any pretense that we can find a viable doctrine of God for our time. Dewart is right in saying that, failing such a doctrine, atheism is the most attractive alternative for the modern intelligence.

There is but one danger in this book: it is so persuasive that it may deceive us into thinking that Christianity's dispute with communism can be resolved by argument or even by "dialogue." It cannot. We learn from the Marxists what we should have known from the Bible: that truth is always found through experience, never through disputation. The question is whether Christianity or communism will contribute more to man's desperate need to "come of age," to his education for reality, to his capacity for accepting unequivocal responsibility for whither history now goes. Jesus said that if we know the truth it will make us free. We must now also recognize that whatever makes us free is *truth*.

4.

A Theology for Our Time

BRIAN WICKER

LESLIE DEWART'S BOOK is the most far-reaching philosophical reappraisal of Catholic belief to have appeared in recent years. It is symptomatic of a shift of emphasis that has begun to appear in Catholic thinking generally—away from "progressive" preoccupations with the modernization of the Church, the liturgy, the parish, the "community" and towards a new way of thinking and feeling about God. The modernization program—at least in terms of books—is wearing thin. Its slogans no longer seem much more relevant than the ones they replaced. They do not offer a satisfactory answer to the question "What the hell does it all mean?" As Sebastian Moore rightly says, in his new book *God is a New Language* (which is another symptom of the same shift in emphasis), "what is *within the circle* (i.e., of progressive theologians) a revolution appears to the wider world to be a purely domestic battle, offering no more than the journalistic interest of a palace revolution." Whereas—the implication is— what is needed is a *real* revolution. Dewart's work is largely subversive: helping to prepare for that revolution and suggesting the outlines of a strategy.

I have some reservations about Dewart's thesis. In one sense I think he goes too far, and almost loses touch with the Church as a

131

community at all—and thus what is being hinted at is liable to become only an intellectual revolution, not one that overturns the world. There is too little link between the theological task of agonizing reappraisal and the political task of agonizing upheaval. And hence there is too little sense of the sheer magnitude of what is being asked for, or the weight of opposition that will be encountered. The theological appraisal could become an escape from history, just as the milieu-Catholicism so ably diagnosed by Carl Amery in his study of the German Church was (and is) an escape from history. And to escape history is to escape God even in the moment of trying to rediscover him.

But there is a positive gain to be set against these losses. This is the possibility that the new theological reappraisal, being concerned with the most basic things of religion as the individual experiences them in himself, might once more bring the radical and the conservative together in a kind of common pursuit. For what lies behind some of the conservative thinking (by no means all) is really a concern with the reality and profundity of our belief in God. It is felt that all the progressive worries about liturgy, community, Church "structures" and social commitment are missing the real thing. The radical like Dewart agrees. There is, of course, a fundamental difference between them. For the God of the conservative is, to the radical, an idol of our own making. Nevertheless, they are at any rate both talking about the same problem—how to speak of God. The danger of this possible line-up is that it will create a new split in the Church— between the modernizing streamliners engaged in their "palace revolution," and the conservative/radical alliance engaged in their exploration of the future of belief. The latter will soon have left behind most of the things that the former are still trying—not terribly successfully—to get started. Once more there is the danger of a rift between bishops and the avant-garde. Just at the moment when the bishops are stepping on to the bottom of the streamlined escalator of structural renewal, the avant-garde are stepping off it at the top, and finding a world there which is as dead as the world they left behind at the bottom. Or is it that they are the ones who are dead—because of the rarefaction of the intellectual atmosphere they breathe up there, in the thin air of Heidegger and Marx? Are they missing the full rich life of parish democracy and the packaged salvation history available in plastic catechetical containers as advertised in the new colored *Universe?* I don't know: all one can do is hope that (as Sebastian Moore puts it) "The experience of being totally at loggerheads on the deepest things of life with people to whom we are bound in a common faith may be as creative as it is painful." Maybe.

Leslie Dewart's book is an attack on the received philosophy of official Catholicism. It rejects both the relevance and, more importantly, the validity of Scholasticism, including that of St. Thomas. Whether this attack is fully merited is too big a question to argue fully here. What matters first of all is that it is a serious, and argued philosophical attack by a fully committed Catholic philosopher. Of course, there have been anti-Scholastic philosophies in the post-Tridentine Church before—that of Newman being, I suppose, the most significant. But none, I think has been so radical in its conclusions, nor so explicitly opposed to the whole tenor of Scholastic thought.

The first place where this attack becomes evident is in the initial discussion of Christian theism and contemporary experience (Chapter 1). Mr. Dewart accepts, in its main drift, Freud's criticism that Christianity as actually experienced in the modern world boils down to a wish-fulfillment or "illusion." Christianity, for the ordinary man, is essentially a "system of doctrines and pledges that on the one hand explains the riddle of the world to him with an enviable completeness, and on the other assures him that a solicitous Providence is watching over him and will make

up to him in a future existence for any shortcomings in this life."
(So Freud.)

Now Freud was a pessimist, who believed that if man cannot
accept this patently infantile worldview he must reconcile himself to living in an unfriendly world where he is an insignificant
and helpless spectator. Modern man cannot be happy, because
God is no longer looking after *him*. Dewart's answer to this is
not that of hellenized Christianity—namely, that man *does* ob-
tain happiness, but not in this world, only in the next. It is that of
a more authenic Christianity—namely, that happiness is not
man's true end. Man's true end is something far more outgoing
than happiness—namely, love. It is only by rejecting both Freud
and hellenized Christianity, with their ethic of happiness as man's
objective, that we can avoid having to admit that the future of
belief is only the future of an illusion:

If the world is envisaged as man's home, and if the purposiveness
of conscious existence is conceived as *being* and not as *being happy*,
the future forecast by Freud for the religious illusion might well
come true—but in the form of a further development of Christian
theism, not in that of its disappearance. [p. 26]

This sentence sums up the whole of Dewart's enterprise. In
order to carry it out he has to explain the true nature of Christian
theism (Chapter 2), and then he has to show how this theism
can be truly said to be present in past theologies, and in the
present life of Christians (even if only distortedly) and may
continue in the future. In other words, he has to work out a
theory of the development of doctrine which is not just the
explicitation of what was once implicit, or the clarification of
what was once but obscurely expressed. It has to be a theory
which allows for the genuinely *new*. And this he holds was never
possible under the hellenistic categories of potency and act, and

134

the epistemological presuppositions of that language. (Thus I think Dewart would not admit the validity of Archbishop Dwyer's remark, in his letter to Fr. Herbert McCabe printed in the March issue of *New Blackfriars,* that while the *substance* of the faith is unchangeable its *expression* "changes as language and manner of thinking change and as the Church sees deeper into and draws out more fully the implications of the Faith once given by God through Christ and his apostles." This is not just an inadequate, or approximate way of putting the matter. It seriously fails to make sense of the idea of development at all. If this is what the doctrine of development means, it does not do the job it sets out to do and fails to account for the evidence which inspired it in the first place. Perhaps it is at points like this that the most difficult and intractable difference between the Catholic radicals and the generality of the bishops makes itself felt: namely, at the level of the most basic philosophical presuppositions and the language which enshrines them. What the latter think to be merely statements of ordinary, orthodox and accepted Catholic belief may to the former be incoherent and unintelligible and in need of total replacement. It is at this level that the most important dialogue needs to take place.)

On the true nature of genuine Christian theism, Dewart is exciting and penetrating. Theism is a kind of mirror-image of atheism. Now there are two kinds of atheism: there is that of (say) Heidegger, which is so absolute that the notion of God ceases even to be worth alluding to. Bothering to deny God explicitly is at least to affirm that he is sufficiently intelligible for it to be worth-while showing that he does not exist. *Absolute* atheism is so uninterested in everything concerned with God that it does not even care to deny him. There is, however, a *relative* atheism—say that of Marx—in which the notion that something is God is intelligible enough. The only question is which thing is God?—and for Marx, man is God. Just as there is an absolute and a relative atheism, there is a relative and an absolute theism. The latter popularly expresses itself in the habit of treating anything that looks as if it might be God with the religious awe and respect due to God. This uncritical respect for anything that smacks of God is unchristian, because it does not distinguish belief in the *true* God from belief in a possibly false God. The Christian's belief in God is not absolute—he must be continually criticising his own belief in order to make sure that it is true. Christian theism is relative, just as Marxist atheism is relative. Both imply the real possibility of belief degenerating into the pursuit of a false God.

Two consequences follow from this, and these constitute the center of Dewart's philosophical enquiry. The first is that the Christian cannot escape the need to have a theory of *truth,* in order to be able to establish that the God he believes in is the true God and not another. The second is that he needs to show that belief in this true God, and all that goes with it, is not so tied to a particular philosophical and cultural system that in order to buy this belief you have to buy some particular cultural package (say the medieval Scholastic package). Chapters 3 and 4 of his book deal respectively with these problems. The first tries to develop a totally non-Scholastic, non-hellenistic theory of truth, and the second tries to show that Christian belief is not tied to any definitive formulations which, of their very nature, commit us to the cultural norms of that formulation. That is to say Christianity is historical, inescapably and to its very roots.

Dewart's theory of truth begins from the premiss that what characterizes the distinctively human form of knowledge is self-consciousness. The hellenistic and Scholastic theory of knowledge does not take this sufficiently into account, or distinguish except in degree the kind of knowledge that an animal can have from that of men. In both cases, according to Scholastic theory, knowledge is essentially a matter of the "intentional appropriation" by the subject of objects other than itself, and, correlatively, of the self-disposition of the self towards other beings. The difference between man and the animals is that man has the capacity—or at any rate a greater capacity—to appropriate the external world by means of concepts which enable him to know the world without actually having to grasp it in his own hands, so to speak. But this capacity does not alter the fact that knowledge consists essentially in the appropriation of external objects. It follows from this theory that *truth* is the conformity of the knowing subject to the object known. It is the adequacy of our representations to the things represented. Now Dewart criticizes this view of truth as being empirically and logically incoherent, in that it asserts a relation of conformity, or adequacy, but makes this relation both (a) "a relation of conformity to the other" and (b) "a relation unilaterally effected by and unilaterally existing in, the knower alone." In other words, it tacitly supposes "that we can conceive and understand knowledge from the outside, as if we could witness from a third, 'higher' viewpoint, the union of two lower things, object and subject" (p. 95). Instead of this theory he proposes another. Man's kind of knowing is not just a more comprehensive understanding, of a larger number of objects, than that of the animals. It is radically different, by virtue of the fact that in knowing anything in the external world man finds that he is aware of his own presence to himself. This presence of man to himself becomes apparent *in* his act of knowing. Now this presence is not just another case of appropriating an object. What the subject is aware of here is not "objectified." Hence, in his most distinctively human act, man does not increase his knowledge by a grasp of more objects, or by the greater complexity of his concepts. His knowledge does not develop by addition, but by *intensification.* This is because his awareness of himself is not an awareness that can increase *quantitatively,* for the object of this awareness is already present as a whole from the first. His

137

awareness of himself can only increase by becoming more intense. And this means that man's knowledge is a continuously developing knowledge. It does not presuppose some fixed and static object known, from which greater knowledge grows by additional steps but which remains substantially immutable in itself as originally presented. On the contrary it suggests a process of intensification in which there is nothing immutable, no definitive truths, nothing that so to speak holds up the process of greater self-awareness, nothing which is not totally surpassed as the process of increasing consciousness proceeds.

It is on the basis of this mechanism of knowledge, and the concomitant notion that truth cannot even be retained unless it continuously grows, that a concept of the development of the Christian truth is possible. The logic of human life is the progressive self-differentiation of man from the reality with which it was "originally continuous and united in un-differentiation." Truth, therefore, is not a matter of a fixed conformity of a static subject to a static object, but of the deepening and intensifying *fidelity* of man to the reality which envelops him.

But man is a social and cultural being, and his grasp of truth is a public rather than a private affair. This means that in the case of Christian doctrine (which is the belief of a society rather than an individual) the true evolution of the Church's teaching is not only possible but inevitable. Just as man is the product of evolution, in the sense that he is the being that *was* an animal but *is not* an animal any more ("Man's present history is an ex-animal one") so present Christian doctrine is the doctrine that *was* the doctrine of the early church but *is not* the doctrine of the early church any more. Its history is totally evolutionary. Christian doctrine cannot help being, at every particular time, cast in a cultural form that is of that time; but it equally cannot help evolving away from that formulation into something new. "The only valid 'criterion' of truth is that it creates the possibility of more truth.

And the most reliable sign that we are coming to the truth is that we are dissatisfied with it" (p. 111). It is not that more *truths*, or new *aspects* of truth, or new ways of expressing the truth appear in Christian history. It is that that very *truth* itself intensifies, and becomes more meaningful, more self-aware.

If Christian truth is evolutionary in this sense, and never complete, then there will always be a certain inadequacy in our concept of God. This *normal* inadequacy comes from the fact that God is necessarily beyond all conceptual formulation, and cannot be grasped in the way that any other object can be grasped. It means that there will always be room for further development of the Christian understanding of God. "There is no foreseeable point at which we shall no longer tend towards God" (p. 126). But this normal inadequacy must be sharply distinguished from an *abnormal* inadequacy, which arises from our side. If the concept of God that we have is in any way false (that is, if we are unfaithful to the true God in any way) then this will adversely affect the development of Christian belief. The static, a-historical hellenistic notion of God, imported into Christianity, did this. For development cannot be halted, only distorted. Historically it took the form of replacing the critical relative theism of Christianity by the absolute theism of a credulous sub-Christian cult. Dr. Dewart expands this point with an important discussion of the distortion of Trinitarian belief in modern times into a kind of *"crypto-tritheism."* He also shows that the Scholastic version of this hellenization was actually the natural progenitor of modern atheism, and led straight to it.

If the hellenistic concept of God is to be rejected, however, we need some indication of an alternative that is adequate to our present, modern experience. In other words we cannot arrive at the outlines of an intelligible concept of God for our time unless we accept that the search for such a concept must begin with the concrete problems of our time, rather than with the abstract

Scholastic questions that were once burning issues but are so no longer. The starting point of such a search must be the recognition that the scholastic presuppositions only allow us to think of God as sending us cryptic messages *about* himself, rather than giving us himself in his actuality. "Belief must bear directly upon the reality of God, not upon words or concepts." It must also bear on man in his contingency. Now today man feels himself to be contingent not because (in the old Scholastic terminology) his essence and his existence are distinct, but because his factual reality "requires him to appear to himself, to come-into-being-in-and-for-himself, to make up his own role as he is suddenly pushed onto the stage of life. In other words, man's contingency is the fact that in order to be he must create himself" (p. 169).

The difference between this religious notion of human contingency and that of a purely humanistic philosophy is that, for the Christian, the self-creation of man by himself is only possible and meaningful because God is himself present within this process. Indeed, this historical process *is* the locus of God's presence to man—there can be no other way in which we can conceive of God. This means that the abstract question of God's *existence*, in the sense that it is posed in (say) the five ways of St. Thomas, is simply irrelevant. It no longer matters, and perhaps no longer even makes sense, to speak as if the question whether God exists or not is the central issue of a Christian metaphysic. It is the *presence* of God to man that is the burning question. In a sense it is a matter of philosophical priorities. If God *is* historically present to man, then the abstract question of whether he *exists* is merely academic. To suppose that before we can say that God is present to man, we have to settle the question whether such a being exists at all is to begin from a particular, and contingent philosophical viewpoint that is no longer relevant to modern experience. (I have argued something like this myself in respect of the notion of the real presence in the eucharist in "The Ministry of the Word," *New Blackfriars,* November 1965.) From the irrelevance of the scholastic notion that God is "a being" who "exists," Dewart goes on to dispose of some other of the "attributes" of God that no longer seem to be relevant or meaningful—his "personality" for example. We no longer think of personality as the pinnacle of a cosmic hierarchy. We see it as that kind of life which, characteristically aspires to go beyond itself. "Personality is what we start from, not what we aspire to, namely, God." Hence God is not an eternal person above history, who has a divine plan for the world. The fundamental relation of man and God is their *mutual* presence *in the conscious creation of the world.* God's omnipotence consists in "the radical openness of nature and history to be fashioned into absolutely anything" (p. 195). Hence the final success of man is not assured in advance by God by any kind of prearranged conclusion. In this sense, Dewart argues, Christianity is like Marxism—only without the latter's surreptitious determinism. (For in Marxism men make their own history, but only within a given environment which conditions them and which they have to accept.) Without God's presence in history Marxism might well be true. God's presence—and *only* his presence—releases man from having to be tied, even in that degree of bondage, to external causality. It makes him really and totally free.

Finally, in view of these radical changes in our concept of God, it may even seem eventually absurd of man to take up an attitude of submission to God. "Christian theism of the future might so conceive God as to find it possible to look back with amusement on the day when it was thought particularly appropriate that the believer should bend his knee in order to worship God" (pp. 203–204).

This last statement may well be one that brings the ordinary, or even the fairly radical Christian, up with a jolt. Is this not just a raising of human pride, which implies a complete rejection of God altogether? What is the point of continuing to talk of God, in the presence of radical reappraisals such as this? (Consistently with his position Dewart does, finally, go on to suggest that the word "God" may indeed be superseded.) Isn't Dewart just a plain atheist who does not, or will not, admit the fact? Now in one sense, he has already forestalled that objection. To label someone an atheist suggests that we are fairly clear about what kind of being he disbelieves in. But Dewart has already shown, convincingly, that this is not so easy as it sounds. Before we can decide whether a man is an atheist or not, we have to know whether the God he disbelieves in is the true God, or just some pseudo God. For example a man who "does not believe in the *existence* of God" may be, not an atheist, but just a Christian philosopher who (like Dewart) does not believe in the intelligibility of the metaphysic which alone gives rise to that kind of abstract question.

All the same, there *is* a real difficulty buried here. Is the choice that Dewart is forcing us to make, between the hellenistic/Scholastic philosophy and that which he advocates the right one? Or—to put the matter more forcefully—is Dewart's alternative fully intelligible? At times he is compelled into locutions that suggest doubts on that score. These cluster around certain key words such as "being," "truth," "reality." We read, for example, "the purposiveness of conscious existence is conceived as *being* and not as *being happy*" (p. 26); "Man can know not only beings, but be-ing; not only being-as-other, but also being-itself" (p. 81); truth "is the fidelity of consciousness to being" (p. 92); "There can be, beyond the totality of all actually existing being, something *present* to us in experience" (p. 177). Now I do not quote these phrases in order to poke fun at them for naïve logical flaws. They appear in a context of intelligent argument, and it would be unfair to pretend that they do not have, in that context, a certain kind of sense. They constitute points at which Dewart tries to show how pieces of the total argument coalesce, or where different threads are pulled together. What I feel hesitant about is whether the argument can in fact, hang together in that kind of way. I am inclined to think that what Dewart's argument reveals is rather a set of paradoxes, and that it is in the gaps opened up by these paradoxes that God is to be found.

One way of putting this is to point out the paucity of concrete examples in the analysis of the key concepts. For example, it is not clear how the notion of *truth* as a fidelity, rather than as a conformity, to the world is related to any specific *truths*. The general direction of Dewart's argument about the nature of truth is, I think sufficiently clear; but how it is to be applied in the analysis of this or that true proposition I am not sure. What sense can be made of the notion that, say, "Mark wrote the earliest gospel" or "John loves Mary" are to be construed, not as statements representing a mind's conformity to the world, but as a person's *fidelity* to it—fidelity being, in this context, precisely something that can grow, become more intense (which, we are told, is the only valid criterion of truth)? John's love for Mary can become more intense: but that the truth enshrined in the statement that he does so itself becomes more intense as his love intensifies is not, to my mind, clear.

What lies behind this problem, I think, is an insufficiently exact conception of the way the development, or intensification of something is actually experienced in perception. It seems to me that to affirm a truth about something within a continuous process of change (e.g., John loves Mary) is necessarily to "freeze" it, and so in a sense distort the continuity of the process itself. Conceptualization is always a breaking up of the continuum of experience into manageable units. This is the very process of thought and expression. "Truth" in the general sense may be capable of a progressive intensification, under the pressure of a progressive intensification, under the pressure of an ever-growing fidelity to reality, but this intensification is only intelligible to us, is only articulable, in terms of particular truths which are severally distinct. Similarly, while it makes sense to speak of the absolute freedom of man, in the presence of God, to make his own future, this future actually confronts us as a set of separate particular possibilities and actions which are already half formed but are as yet uncompleted. My future is, so to speak, already structured (and to that extent closed) by what is visible of it in my present situation, and to that extent I can only go on into it along certain tracks. (To do otherwise would not be to continue the present in a different, unexpected way: it would be to abolish the connectedness of events altogether.)

My own view therefore is that the project of totally replacing the static Scholastic philosophy by a purely dynamic, historical one is a philosophical impossibility. That there is a certain validity in it is, I think, undeniable. But the notion that experience is reducible under one comprehensive and self-consistent view is mistaken. Human experience is fundamentally paradoxical. It is, so to say, "faulted" and it is along the fault lines that we find exposed the signs of God's presence. He lives where the two systems meet but do not merge. And since, along that edge there is only a line—which is not a thing, or even a space where there might be a thing, this paradoxicality reveals God's *absence* as a particular being but his presence as a hope for a different mode of experience, to be found perhaps in a new heaven and a new earth which is free from this kind of faulting.

This conclusion, if true, is important in a practical way, since it has direct practical, even political implications. For one of the urgent questions that Dewart's thesis raises is whether there is anything to distinguish Christian theism as he envisages it from (for instance) the "total secular redemption" of man by his own efforts, as has been envisaged by Raymond Williams in *Modern*

Tragedy. At a first glance, it seems hard to see what difference there is between man's self-redemption in the light of God's historical presence, and his self-redemption through a purely secular-humanist revolution. Furthermore, both conceptions seem to suffer from the same kind of logical and philosophical flaws.[1] This problem becomes acute if we take seriously Dewart's assertion that "there is no foreseeable point at which we shall no longer *tend* towards God" (p. 126). I am not sure if this means that there is no longer any sense to the idea of an end of history, a final winding-up of the empirical cosmos. An important article by Dewart, on the eschatological meaning of celibacy and its diminishing significance for a world which no longer expects "that the parousia should be . . . a discrete event which begins to occur at a certain moment of Aristotelean time" seems to suggest that in fact there is no end at all to history.[2] The *parousia*, on this view, is simply "God's self-extrusion into the world, as the fulfilment of God's gracious incarnation . . . [it is] the presence of Christ insofar as this presence is historical, transforming, progressive and evolving."

This view seems to me inadequate. It is only on the basis of some kind of cosmic ending (which would of course be also a transfiguration of the cosmos, an inauguration, a rebirth from a true death of history) that there seems to be any possibility of a reconciliation between the two incompatible conceptual systems that (as I see it) we cannot do without, despite their mutual incompatibility. The paradox of experience itself demands this "catastrophic" conclusion. In the perspective of the present order, in which we find, sacramentally, the beginning of this end, it seems possible to distinguish total secular redemption from total

1. For an examination of these flaws in Raymond Williams' book see Walter Stein's articles in *New Blackfriars,* February and March 1967, and *Slant,* June/July, 1967.
2. *Commonweal,* April 22, 1966.

Christian redemption only if, on the stage of history itself, we can find some distinctive structure that already belongs to this future. The Church, a body in some sense within the greater society of mankind, but empirically distinguishable within that larger grouping, is the only possible candidate for this role. Thus one consequence of my criticism of Dewart's philosophical enterprise is that he has not, explicitly, dealt with the problem of the future structure and role of the Church itself. He is right, of course, to insist on the need to work out a contemporary concept of God, and to emphasize that this has not been sufficiently dealt with in recent theology. But there cannot, in the last analysis, be any distinction, even methodologically, between envisaging a true and relevant modern concept of God and envisaging a relevant concept of the Church.

5.

Dewart's
Reconceptualization
of Catholic Belief in God

ARTHUR GIBSON

IT WOULD BE a misfortune if Leslie Dewart's exciting insights and speculations in *The Future of Belief* were to be obscured by any "To your tents, O Israel!" reaction to his preliminary critique. Perhaps he has wielded the scalpel of his devastatingly precise prose a little close to the bone; perhaps he has seemed to be as hasty and sweeping as Roboam and to convey to an already startled Scholasticism the impression that if it had been beaten with whips before, he would now beat it with scorpions. Perhaps, above all, his preliminary critique manages to fall most unfortunately midway between a general review not requiring meticulousness and exhaustiveness of detail and a thorough-going specialized study providing the necessary qualifications of some of the criticisms. But the opening words of the book clearly identify it as an essay in meaningful communication in our present day and in no sense a systematic critical communication or survey of the past. It is an essay in speculative theology, not a critique of

147

the thought of the past. "This book attempts to sketch an approach . . . to the problem of integrating Christian theistic belief with the everyday experience of comtemporary man" (p. 1). Notoriously the prophet is a poor archivist and the examiner of broad horizons does not always do perfect justice to the intricate patterning of the individual leaf (or even forest!). But this by no means invalidates the broader insight. This book is primarily important as a call to Christian theists to transcend their present absolute (and therefore idolatrous) theism in order to ensure Christianity a future as a relevant articulation of ultimate human experience; the overall cultural situation of man is changing ineluctably, and the human mode of articulation of Christian theism must grow with the "phylogenetic development" of the race or risk becoming irrelevant.

Even when Dr. Dewart is conducting his critical examination of the past (which occupies 170 pages, as against 45 pages of "tentative and exploratory" speculation), he is examining the past in the present with a view to the future. His chief and recurrent call is for a *dehellenization* of epistemology, metaphysics and theology, which will signify "in positive terms, the conscious creation of the future of belief." Dehellenization in epistemology is basic to dehellenization in the other two realms mentioned; and this dehellenization of epistemology Dewart describes as an approach to man's intellectual life which would see that life not as "a subject's assimilation of objects to itself (and of itself to objects), but the emergence of a self as it becomes present to itself by self-differentiating itself from the totality of being." He argues that this approach would entail an understanding of "human psychism not as the operation of a faculty of a substance which would alone exercise primary existence, but as a reality which constitutes the very being of man . . . the mind's self *differentiation* of itself out of a reality with which it was originally continuous and united in un-differentiation" (pp.

90–91). Dehellenization in metaphysics would involve a radical departure from post-Parmenidean Greek metaphysics which "identified the necessity of being and the necessity of intelligibility through the identity of being and intelligibility (p. 155), and Dr. Dewart sketches the resulting situation as one in which "ontological enquiry would no longer be the investigation of *being as such*. . . . It would be no more and no less than the study of reality as such, that is, without abstraction from its reality, concreteness, immediacy, actuality, historicity and factuality" (p. 169). Dehellenization in theology would involve an escape from the notion that any "given concept of God can be the unique and necessary concept of God required by Christian belief" (p. 131) and would free theology from unprofitable concern with demonstration of the existence of God so that full attention could be devoted to "showing how God *in his reality* is *present* to human experience. . . . Such a God, however, would not be even partially that of Greek metaphysics. For this would be an integrally *Christian* philosophy. Its God would be wholly and exclusively the Christian God" (p. 170).

The threefold dehellenization here called for is clearly a process involving a drastic passage from staticity of conception to dynamism at all three levels. Dr. Dewart pinpoints the threefold damage done to Christianity by hellenization as the introduction into Christianity of "the ideals of immutability, stability and impassibility as perfections that all Christians and Christianity as a whole should strive for, since these were the typical and central perfections of God himself" (p. 134), and he concludes that "the development of dogma stimulated and made possible by the hellenization of Christianity meant . . . its petrification" (p. 135). For it involved the canonization not only of an identifiable conceptualization of belief in the Christian God, but also, and more drastically, a canonization of a *certain kind of approach,* the static approach. But, as Dewart points out in his admirable gloss of the "second Sinaitic commandment," we "cannot without idolatry believe in anything or anyone else in the same way in which we believe in God" (p. 70).

Dewart's 45 pages of exciting theological speculation cover seven main points: the being and existence of God, the personality of God, the omnipotence of God, the eternity of God, the basis of man's religious relations with God, the supernatural character of God and the name of God. The remarks he makes concerning our use of the name of God "if not with recklessness, at least with some abandon" (p. 215) and his suggestion of a "special place for *silence* in *discourse* about God" (p. 214) should recommend themselves not only as an ideal in the moral-religious order but as a conscious methodology as well, to anyone familiar with Rilke's poignant words about *"ausmalen"* (in paintings generally and quite specifically in the God-dimension) as a technique of highlighting. His speculations on five of the other points are equally stimulating and thought-provoking.

It is only his speculations on the first point, the being and existence of God, which give rise to some hesitation and even reservation. His beginning remark is surely unexceptionable as such: "The Christian theism of the future might not conceive God as *a being*" (p. 173). For, as Bishop Robinson has eloquently pointed out in some detail, a plethora of present theological and practical difficulties has arisen from this illegitimate importation of the angle of vision of geometry into theology. But Dewart goes on to say: "I place the stress not merely on the indeterminate article *a* but also on the substantive *being*" (p. 173). There can still be total agreement with Dr. Dewart, providing he adheres rigidly to this *substantive* notion of being; but in his further development of this speculation, he seems to neglect unduly the participial sense of being or to wish to transcend even it in his concept of God. For he speaks of an epistemological underpinning for the transcending leap involved: "If reality is not assumed to be constitued by intelligibility . . . reality can no longer be identified with that-which-is (which is the usual meaning of being, *ens*)" (p. 174). It may be the usual meaning, but it is not the only possible one! It is precisely the hellenization of Christian thought that has promoted this meaning to the status of the usual meaning. But one might wish that in quite rightly overleaping the hellenistic substantive notion of being in reference to God, Dewart did not overleap, or at least create the impression he was overleaping, the participial sense as well. Between the hellenist or hellenized substantive "being" and Dr. Dewart's "open background against which [man] becomes conscious of transcendence . . . beyond man, beyond transcendence and therefore beyond being . . . God . . . should therefore not be conceived as being. . . . What the religious experience of God discloses is a reality *beyond* being" (pp. 174–75); one might wish to insert a third notion, the notion of participial being.

Thus Dewart's sentence above might be examined thus: God . . . should therefore not be conceived as being in the substantive sense, whether as a granular kernel of being or as an undular but still identifiably substantive stream of totality of being—agreed without reservation; God . . . should therefore not be conceived as being participially understood—a distinction must be made: if any faintest notion of substantive granulation is being surreptitiously introduced (in the form of an embryonic notion that if God is, he must be something or at least some way), then again enthusiastic agreement; if, however, any such impermissible substantive nuance be entirely expunged from the statement, then one cannot so enthusiastically agree; indeed one must assume an attitude of extreme vigilance. And this vigilance seems fully justified when we read a few pages later that "if God does not come into being, then he is not a being, and if he is not a being, then he does not exist" (p. 184), or that he is "a reality beyond the totality of being. . . ." (p. 177). One would wish that Dewart's admira-

ble insight into the dynamic of human beings, which enables him
to write the excellent sentence "Consciousness develops . . . not as
an additional perfection of a faculty of being. . . ." (p. 91) and
to come out sharply against any notion of consciousness as something possessed by some anteriorly constituted substance, could
have been extended to the ontological area as well. It is those
damnable essences at work again.

Being is conceived as a predicate of some anteriorly constituted
reality; being is conceived as a perfection which can be superadded to some reality more basic than beings; being is conceived
as one delimited area of dimension of a reality that transcends
being. And the door is open to nothingness as a reality. This
consequence of the reification of being, of the granulation and
substantivization of being, is surely the profoundest error with
which Christian philosophy was infected upon contact with hellenism. It is curious that one who wishes to transcend hellenization should fall into it. I am sure Dr. Dewart did not intend to; it
may be that he has not; I can only say that he certainly appears
to have done so.

Surely the transcendence of God is not to be sought in his
escape from the entire dimension of this essentially secondary
and fortuitous predicate but rather in his absolute identity with
this primary power. This absolute and exhaustive identity can
only be expressed, it seems to me, in human terms by recourse to
the participle, the verbal adjective whose ultimate derivation is
from a pure-action verb and whose entire coloring is descriptive
rather than definitive. Substantives are latecomers in the gram-
mar of sound ontology; the verb is primary. But among verbs,
there are those which are only relatively primary ("knowing" is
absolutely primary for the realm of consciousness, as Dewart so
admirably points out, but it is not absolutely primary), and there
is a verb which is absolutely primary. The verb TO BE is that
verb over against which we can set validly no other verb which

would articulate an action different from and privative of the action expressed by TO BE.

This is a point of vital importance in a dialogue between Christian theists and Marxist atheists. To free God from the cramping substantive tether of *a* reified being is one thing and will certainly aid the dialogue precisely by abolishing the unprofitable argument about the existence of God in a context that presupposes him to be a bit of being, a possible to be raised to the level of an actual by some kind of demonstration or proof. But to project God beyond the boundaries of being, where being is understood participially, is quite another thing and could lead to serious misunderstandings and equally unprofitable apparent reconciliations.

A Marxist recently said to me: "If by God you simply wish to indicate the limitless possibilities and horizons of the future, there would be no difficulty in our accepting that sort of term." Dr. Dewart's "reality beyond the totality of being" which "reveals itself by its *presence"* seems to me to indicate an opening-up of the horizons in no uncertain terms but an opening not onto a transcendent creator but rather onto a hyperontological ultimate whose self-revelation, far from being effected ultimately via being, is in fact hampered by being. The consequential Marxist has utterly eliminated staticity in any sense from his world picture; the consequential Parmenidean has in practice eliminated all dynamism.

But the fruitful ground of dialogue between Marxists and Christians surely lies not in the context of a Christian abandonment of all staticity but rather in an abandonment of Platonic staticity via a full explicitation of the consequences of the notion of participial being and a concomitant recognition of the Marxist's part of the requirement of some ultimate ontological static principle, some fulcrum for the spiral of becoming. That fulcrum is being participially articulated, the ontological ultimate, the truest of all our inadequate names for the Unnameable. The Real who makes his presence felt to man is indeed "no supreme being who stands at the summit of the hierarchy of being" (p. 177) but neither is he a migrant from any outer depths beyond being (I am perfectly aware that Dr. Dewart is not intending any crude—or subtle, for that matter—spatialization on this whole argumentation; neither am I!). He is precisely the primary and absolute power of that realm which we call being (here using the word in still another sense!) and which only our inveterate itch to conceptualize prods us to call a realm at all, since we can set nothing whatever over against it as genuinely delimiting. We live in a closed universe! The sense of evolution is not properly expressed, even pictorially, in the ontological sphere, as an indefinite expansion of horizon but rather as a progressive intensification of (com) presence, a convolution. But participial being does not involve any of the intolerable consequences in the moral order of humanism which ensue in a Parmenidean substantive presupposition in regard to being. A supreme being substantively conceived as the ultimate vertical master is intolerable to the Marxist atheist and should be to any decent Christian theist. But participial being provides a fulcrum for the centripetal spiral without in any way inhibiting the ever-emerging and ever-intensifying perfection (i.e., being) of the ontological manifold constituting that spiral.

It seems to me that the basic flaw in the Marxist materialist atheist is the illicit transference of a yen for purely spatial indefinite expansion, normal in its own sphere, into the domain of consciousness and interiority where it becomes a centrifugal force frustrating the centripetal inclination normal here. The contribution of the theist can most properly be a more adequate enucleation and elucidation of this centripetal moment via a clearer portrayal of ultimate participial being. For the Being I have here attempted to describe would attract substantive beings without violating or infringing their substantiality; and it would be borne in upon these substantive beings by the presence of this Being that their highest perfection (and bliss) lies in a centripetal transcendence of the narrow bounds of their own substantiveness. The real meeting ground must be in the ontological area. I believe that Dr. Dewart's articulation of God would benefit by attention to these observations.

6.

Theism Today and Tomorrow

JOHN W. M. VERHAAR, S.J.

THE FACT THAT ATHEISM is virtually not found in non-Christian cultures is so significant that it seems incredible that this fact had not been realized more clearly before. Is it not possible that after the Second Vatican Council's *peccavimus* in our approach to the Reformation we may also have to beat our breasts in approaching the non-Christians in our Christian milieu? To those preoccupied with the uniqueness of Christianity as the *signum levatum inter nationes* this may seem like overstepping the boundaries of admissible compromise: it may even seem that one would in so doing be trying to safeguard Christianity by diluting it beyond recognition so as to communicate with unbelievers on something like a common ground. In fact, Mascall, in what is possibly a too massive attack on "religionless Christianity" and "Christian atheism," has summarized what must be the objection felt by many: that instead of converting the world to Christianity, we are converting Christianity to the world.[1] Yet it

1. E. L. Mascall, *The Secularization of Christianity*, New York and London, 1966, *passim*, e.g. pp. 101–102.

is by no means obvious that anything so cataclysmic is necessarily taking place in all cases of modern radical theology. As regards Catholic theology, which is our concern now, we should realize that there can never be any undue compromise in admitting previous failings. And perhaps the most important single theological issue in Catholic theology, possibly hardly less than in Protestant modern thinking, is that of the problem of God. If that problem does indeed have the kind of background that must be subjected to scrutiny in the first place, then what we should be aiming at is a new Christian theism.

This is precisely what Leslie Dewart's *The Future of Belief* attempts to do. Dewart's book is a detached, balanced, and thoroughly scholarly work. In line with this comment, also, I should like to remark that the book is indeed "radical," but not in the first place, and perhaps not at all, in the sense of "left wing" or "iconoclastic"; the book is radical in the quite literal and levelheaded sense that it goes to the very roots of some of the problems of theism in the modern conception of the Catholic faith.

The principal merit of the book, in my opinion, is the coherent and expert exposition of how it has been possible at all for Catholic theology, even until quite recently, to get so completely out of touch with the spirit of the times. The fact itself of this alienation has been noted often before; in explanation it has been pointed out that in the twentieth century we can hardly be expected to benefit by allegiance to a theology, however brilliant, of the thirteenth. The explanation, however, has to go far beyond exposing a seven-century gap. Nothing becomes necessarily untrue or irrelevant because it was said long ago, even if one accepts, as Dewart does, the need for development and reinterpretation. Dewart's main point is actually not so much our allegiance to Scholastic thought, but Scholastic allegiance to hellenic thought. Then, again, that Scholasticism has been heavily indebted to Greek philosophy has also been known all along. However, the *charge* of hellenization of Christian dogma has been pressed almost exclusively in Reformation theology, already in the nineteeth century, notably by von Harnack. And in view of this fact, which, to my knowledge, has never been adequately met by Catholic theology, it is the more interesting to note that Dewart opposes it. That is, he does not think that the hellenization of Christian dogma was wrong; all he claims is that it has been unduly perpetuated. Thus the "perennial philosophy" of Scholasticism is not so much the problem as the symptom of a problem more basic. Therefore Dewart's program is a dehellenization of dogma rather than a denunciation of Scholasticism. He regrets that, put this way, his program is a negative one; but he is enough of a realist to see that that is where we have to begin. Whereupon he himself sets an example with some highly interesting and inspiring attempts at rejuvenation of Catholic thinking.

But this is not yet clear enough, as a representation of what the author is saying. From the preceding it might still appear as if we are mainly concerned with an updating of theology in, let us say, the way of an adaptation. However, the issue is not in the first place theology, but that on which theology is a reflection: the faith. Second, the word "adaptation" might be misunderstood as meaning that only marginal changes might suffice to bring out better the immutable revealingness of the core. All this, however, would imply that Christian dogma is a monolithic whole, which, being presented to the faithful, would have to be "integrated" into his "previous" human experience, even though it might have to be done with certain fringe adaptations to make the integration possible. This supposition would imply that dogma, or, say, the articles of faith, would open the way, when assented to, to God in Christ. This position, however, is not accepted by the author. On the one hand, he does not deny that a certain conceptualization is necessary; indeed, he thinks it is of the essence of

159

faithful consciousness. On the other hand, however, he insists that such a conceptualization is not something *in between* human consciousness and divine revelation, but part of that consciousness itself. If one were to think (as some might) that this is just another version of rationalism and/or semi-Pelagianism (of the kind, say, rejected by the Council of Orange), that would be to miss the author's point completely. It would be like applying the Thomistic concept of "nature" (as correlative with "supernature") to Augustine's concept of "nature" (in the "same" correlation), which would of course be tantamount to making Augustine a Pelagianist. For Augustine considers nature as already ordinated towards the supernatural, a thing Thomas otherwise perfectly well recognized.[2] Similarly, Dewart is not speaking of consciousness in a manner philosophically meant to be a preliminary understanding for the kind of consciousness that we call the faith; he is speaking only of the latter, not, therefore, the consciousness of God's salvific presence *through* the truths of the faith proposed to him for acceptance, but those truths *in* God's presence and involvement in his personal and communal life. To point this out seems useful to preclude unnecessary misunderstandings concerning Dewart's position.

In short: for Dewart the faith is an articulated consciousness or self-awareness, which differentiates the self and all the factors of experience in faithful belief in God. It follows, therefore, that the concept of God has to be in harmony with the totality of experience. This is not to say that Dewart has been treading the weary way of nineteenth-century Protestant liberal theology all over again in a Catholic manner; or, it is not that God is degraded to human needs, let alone to human demands. It is, on the contrary, to say that God's involvement in history is incarnate in the way this human history develops. When God reveals

2. Cf. H. de Lubac, *Le mystère du surnaturel,* Paris, 1965, pp. 41 ff.

himself to twentieth-century man, it is hard to see why twentieth-century consciousness has to be stretched on a Procrustus bed seven centuries long, or even more than three times as long if one takes into account the hellenic foundations of Scholastic thought.

The hellenic background and foundation of traditional theology looms much larger than can be seen in medieval Scholasticism only. An illuminating example of this is given by Dewart when speaking of Freud's attitude to religion.[3] When Freud stated that religion is an illusion, this did not necessarily mean, even for Freud himself, that religion is an error. He defined an illusion as a belief inspired by wish-fulfillment. However, the epistemological impact is not important here, since Freud was against religion anyway; but a more important reservation made by Freud is that he was speaking about the religious experience of "ordinary man"; and then it can indeed hardly be denied that religious goals have often been motivated by what really amounts to a refusal to shoulder personal responisbility.[4] More important is a second reservation made by Freud, that is, where he explains why, in his view, man would feel the need of such illusions at all. It is because that is the way man counterbalances the threats of a cruel world. However, says Dewart, there is evidently, but also quite gratuitously, a distinct pessimism in such an anthropomorphic conception of the "ill will" of the world towards man; that pessimism, according to Dewart, is the heritage of Greek thinking, to which Freud was also otherwise so heavily indebted. The salient point of Freud's negative attitude, the author goes on to say, towards religion is not therefore his

3. See also Paul Ricoeur, "The Atheism of Freudian Psychoanalysis," *Concilium*, vol. 16 (*Is God Dead?*), New York and London, 1966, pp. 59–72.

4. This is a theme dear to recent Reformation theology; see John A. T. Robinson, *The New Reformation?*, Philadelphia and London, 1965.

failure to recognize a harmonious, instead of a distorted, type of Christian experience, but rather that there is nothing obvious in the *Weltanschauung* from which he started out in the first place. Consequently, instead of picturing Freud as inadmissibly radical with regard to religious experience in general, what should be clearly recognized is that at least in one important facet of his theory he was not radical enough. There is of course a remarkable parallel between Freud and Marx in that the latter found religion to be "opium to the people" because it frustrated, in his view, legitimate concerns for human happiness during this life, by relegating all those concerns to the hereafter.[5] Have not exploited workers been too long and too often told that this life is a vale of tears and that it was their duty to accept what apparently for them was the will of God? One need not in any way be unaware of the mystery of suffering, let alone of its redemptive function, to contest the view that "a vale of tears" is the best theological characterization of human life on earth.

I will bypass the issue whether the last example does not at least go back as much to a perhaps too other-worldly ideal of Christian perfection as noticeable in the Church's history of this ideal; or, the source of the pessimism underlying such an ideal is perhaps not so easy to trace back to the typically hellenic pessimism as in the example of Freud. However, we can afford to bypass this issue in favor of one to be found even on a deeper level, and one expounded by Dewart. It is something apparently so innocuous as the conception of *happiness,* which, according to Dewart, is as typically hellenic as it is arbitrary when abstracted from the hellenic frame of reference. That conception could

5. Marx's metaphysics goes deeper than this more humanistic and pastoral aspect (the latter of which is of course no concern of his), i.e., Marx wanted the unity of Man and Nature to replace that of God and Man; see Gaston Fessard, S.J., "The Theological Structure of Marxist Atheism," *Concilium,* etc. (see above, note 3), pp. 7–24.

easily lead to what Dewart calls "spiritual hedonism." If, as is done in the theology of St. Thomas, happiness is taken to be man's perfection, there is the danger that, as Dewart phrases it, man's perfection is not so much *to be happy* as *to be*. This somewhat obscure statement is clarified when we follow the author in the elaboration of this conception. The traditional "beatific vision" is again a sort of intermediate entity between man and God; or, perhaps more accurately, the conceptions of God and man find another conception of "beatitudo" wedged between them in a manner not quite obviously called for. Here is a most interesting parallel with the notion of the faith as supposedly intermediate between man and God: just as certain conceptualizations of faithful consciousness (say, the articles of the Creed) are not *mediating between* believing man and the God he believes in, so also happiness, whatever its conception, is not (necessarily) in between man and the God he loves.[6]

The parallelism of truth and happiness is of great importance, and not for historical reasons alone. If it is indeed possible for a believer to love the gift more than the giver, is it not also, and quite analogously, true that the "appropriation" of the faith in certain fixed and readily "available" conceptualizations could turn the experience of the faith into a personal accomplishment, a "possession" to which the believer might feel (even though perhaps largely unconsciously) entitled, or which he might even use as an inquisitorial weapon against his brothers in Christ?

The author is saying that the hellenic frame of reference has

6. A folkloristic story recounted by Dewart illustrates the latter point better than any theoretical exposition. It tells about an angel who, carrying a pail of water and a flaming torch, was asked by a saint passing by what he was going to do. The angel replied that he was going to set fire to the castles of heaven and extinguish the flames of hell; and that then he would be curious to see who would love God more: the blessed or the doomed.

led to a theology of dualism; the dualism between knower and known, and the dualism between pessimism of human forlornness and the urge for happiness. It has of course been attempted to overcome these dualisms by means of sophisticated gradations of intermediacy. But this obviously is not to overcome the dualism, but to refine it to the point where it would be less easily recognized and do proportionately more harm. In Scholastic theological dimensions this concretely means that the living faith has been inhibited by the intermediacy of monolithic truths, with more concern for their immutability and over-all validity than for their relevance to certain types of consciousness in certain ages and cultures; while the love for God has been obstructed by a concern for happiness which not only is unnecessary as a bridge and harmful as a gap, but also harbors not a few psychological problems. The first inhibition arises out of the kind of doubt which has nothing to do with the inevidence of the faith or its essentially numinous character, and therefore out of what at least objectively must be branded as unfaithfulness; while the second emerges from a pessimism which is in its roots fatalistic and unrelated to the mysteries of both iniquity and suffering, basically at variance with love and therefore at least objectively selfish. With regard to the first issue we might say (as Dewart does) that ideally we are not permitted to have faith in faith, we are allowed and privileged—to have faith in God alone; and likewise we must never fall in love with happiness, not even the happiness God is granting us; we must love God alone. This is not to say that the faith is not certain, but that its certainty does not have to consist, and must never exclusively consist, in making it reduplicative; likewise the claim is not that we do not find happiness in the love of God, but that this happiness must never be allowed to make its own demands because then it will be impossible from the start to overcome our selfishness.

THE HELLENIC VIEW OF REALITY

While the preceding explorations into some backgrounds of hellenic thinking have reached deep into the less accessible, because less obviously problematic, issues of Catholic theology, the more explicit problem of Christian theism should also come up for discussion.

The problem of the existence of God, according to Dewart, has always been outlined against the background of the problem of the existence of objects. The negative side of this is that hellenic and Scholastic thinking have, on the whole, contributed little to the understanding of man. The ultimate basis of the problem of knowledge Dewart finds in the Parmenidean principle of the equivalence of being and intelligibility. However, being had, in Greek thought, always been considered as necessary, and that is where, obviously, Scholasticism had to introduce a reservation. It was not that the Greeks were unaware of contingency, but that was put down to chance circumstances which in the last analysis are reducible to the notions of matter and (later) potency. Scholasticism therefore, pressed on the one hand by the Greek notion of the necessity of being, and on the other by the inevitability of reserving necessary being for God alone, found the ingeniously simple solution that created beings, although contingent, were at least necessary with regard to their intelligibility, that is, their essence. Therefore, created beings could have a necessary intelligibility and yet a contingent existence. The retrenchment of necessity to intelligibility or essence of course necessitated the real distinction between essence and existence. For obvious reasons this distinction was not to be held for God. Dewart feels that had Thomas retained the conception of contingency of created beings but abandoned the Parmenidean principle, the history of Catholic thought might have been different. Ockham of course was to draw the conclusion that no amount of knowledge about the essence of an object could enlighten us as to its existence. From the ensuing doubt, i.e., that we can never be sure that anything actually exists, it follows obviously that, unless the existence of God be demonstrable from the identity of his essence and existence, that existence is as problematic as that of the creatures; and even more so seeing that, unlike creatures, God is not empirically intuitable. This, in the philosophy of Descartes, ultimately led to the *a priori* certainty of God's existence, on the part of unbelievers to skepticism and later to atheism; and, eventually, in the Catholic camp to fideism. Once agnosticism came in, on the part of unbelievers, concerning the existence of a God of whom they nevertheless had a sure concept, the way was open for anyone who discovered an empirical *substitute,* and a meaningful one, for that same concept of God, which, even though it was not subject to the same doubt as was his existence, yet failed to be meaningful enough to carry conviction. That is why most of modern atheism is a "relative" atheism (a concept to be explained below). Dewart, quoting Hinners,[7] claims that Marx, who interpreted Hegel in going back to the old Greeks, should have interpreted the Greeks by tracing the logical consequences of the Parmenidean postulate to Hegel. From that type of metaphysics stemmed absolute theism; from absolute theism it had to come to atheism. Also the antinomy between rationalism and fideism is to be traced back, according to Dewart, to the same hellenic false start. And thus, says Dewart, it is understandable that Vatican I, in an otherwise entirely justified concern to rule out fideism, had to wind up in the conclusion that it was a matter of *faith* that the existence of God was *rationally* demonstrable.

7. Richard Hinners, *Ideology and Analysis: A Rehabilitation of Metaphysical Ontology,* New York, 1966, p. 131.

Dewart is actually pointing out not so much what Greek philosophy was saying as what it was implying: the necessity of reality. He nowhere notes that at least in modern Thomism the notion of necessity as transcendentally convertible with being makes contingent being at least *analogically* "necessary." I assume the reason for this is Dewart's qualms about the analogy of being itself (in one place he notes that though in a system of *predication* it might make sense, for an *understanding* of the problem of God it is inhibiting), especially because it so easily would lead to absolute theism. However, we shall return to Dewart's analyses of the Greek and Scholastic notions and treatment of being later, and for the moment it is necessary to explain what "absolute" and "relative" mean, for Dewart, in the context of theism and atheism.

THEISM AND ATHEISM AS ABSOLUTE AND RELATIVE

The distinctions conveyed here are philosophically of great importance, and we shall attend to those alone for the moment; theologically, however, I shall have more comments later. Briefly, then, as Dewart explains it, *absolute atheism* is the type of atheism in which God lacks all reality; it implies a theoretical indifference with regard to theism. According to some, this type is found in Heidegger and Merleau-Ponty. *Relative atheism* is roughly that Maritain calls "positive" atheism (a coincidence not mentioned by Dewart): it is a concept of and interest in the problem of theism, but bent backwards to some mundane reality, mostly man; it is an "inverted" theology, and it is found in Marx, Nietzsche, Freud, Sartre. The alternative values with regard to which the traditional Christian God is supposed to be competitive and therefore has to be "killed," are, respectively, the unity of man and nature, individual human greatness, psychological integration, and freedom. In relative atheism the non-existence of God is not a beginning, but a conclusion. The existence of God is denied because it is found to be metaphysically, scientifically, logically, psychologically, or (especially) morally impossible.[8] Relative atheism, therefore, is "conditional" atheism. It is, in the term of de Lubac, not so much atheism as antitheism. This might induce some thinkers to speak of that type of atheism as crypto-theism. While from a purely systematic point of view this would be true (the term "inverted" theology comes to much the same, and also *mutatis mutandis* Mircea Eliade would speak of "crypto-religious behavior" on the part of modern secularized man [9]), to insist on this, says Dewart, would inhibit not only dialogue with atheists but also the failings of Christian practice, not coming up to the ideals of Christian belief. In this connection Dewart concentrates especially on Marxism, and suggests that to say that Marxism is a theism unaware of its own nature would be to overlook the fact that Christianity has been all too often a humanism unaware of its own nature; this, however, has not been in general a point the Marxists have insisted upon.

The inadequacy of traditional forms of Christian theism here at issue is then, according to Dewart, that it has been largely an absolute theism. While absolute atheism is the belief that nothing could be possibly God, *absolute theism* is the kind of thinking inclined towards the belief that anything is apt to be God. It is therefore close to idolatry. It appropriates divine reality within the dangerously distorting confines of human arbitrariness, degrades God accordingly, adduces premature solutions to establish

8. See also John A. T. Robinson, *The New Reformation?*, pp. 106–22, where the traditional conception of God is found to be "intellectually superfluous," "emotionally dispensable," and "morally intolerable."

9. Mircea Eliade, *The Sacred and the Profane: The Nature of Religion*, New York, 1961, pp. 201–13.

a supposedly indispensable stability of what is in fact an over-organized articulation of the faith, and is basically a most serious oversight of another and more important tradition in the Christian doctrine of God, that of the Pseudo-Dionysian tradition of the *docta ignorantia,* of the *via eminentiae* of the Thomistic *triplex via,* and of the tradition of the great mystics of the Church, for example St. John of the Cross in his theology of the *nada.* Here is, therefore, says the author, where relative atheism, however much antitheistic in effect, should begin to appear strangely familiar to the Christian, induce him to an examination of his conscience, and to dialogue with at least the relative atheists of whatever color. He will then arrive at a *relative theism.*

What relative atheism should do for us in our actual Christian (contemporary) experience, says Dewart, is that our respect for God and a healthy fear of anything approaching idolatry imply a true and genuine *concern* for the truth of our belief in God; this *practically* implies, of sheer necessity, a certain amount of disbelief. Note that what the author is speaking about is a *concern* for the truth of our belief, a *practical* attitude, therefore, and not the *theoretical* concern leading to the need for *reduplicative* certainty. This view then ties up almost organically with that other one of Dewart's, that we should beware of a faith which relies on itself instead of on God. The traditional concern for reduplicative certainty, even when triggered by an otherwise legitimate fear of fideism, should never lead us, unawares, into faith in faith; while the practical concern with the truth of our belief in God is ever to assert our contingency in the face of his presence, a healthy fear, therefore, that God might somehow become our-"possession" (which would be the same as idolatry).[10] It is all

10. What Dewart means by concern, therefore, is *vigilance,* and the "disbelief" or "doubt" in the *practical* sense is a suspicion of the human tendency to draw within the sphere of personal human accomplishment

too easy for man to end up by claiming to know too much about God.

ANALOGY, TRANSCENDENCE, AND PRESENCE

Supposing for a moment that the Scholastic thinker were to share with Dewart the notions of relative and absolute theism at least according to what they mean, he would, of course, promptly plead not guilty of the latter by pointing out his doctrine of the analogy of being. Dewart does not say much about that theory, beyond the important comment already alluded to, that as a manner of *predication* it is no doubt defensible, but that it cannot be dovetailed into the *understanding* of the God of Christianity. In terms of contemporary experience it may even distort Christian understanding of God: although the analogy of being does not imply, in any sense, that God is the *apex mundi*, yet in terms

what can never belong there. That is what makes the *attitude* advocated by Dewart entirely different from fideism. The faith is "reasonable" in more than one sense: (a) that it, although transcending reason, is in no way counter to reason; (b) that there are, as traditional terminology has it, the "external signs of credibility;" (c) that it is possible to interconnect, to a certain extent, the truths of the faith, *"aliquam Deo dante intelligentiam"* (D. 1796), so as to arrive at a greater understanding of the faith, *"eamque fructuosissimam"* (*ibid.*). Dewart simply presupposes, (a) among other things by emphasizing the inevidence of the faith, and (b) in insisting that the faith be meaningful for these times. He is mainly concerned with (c) by eliminating anachronisms in the faith in the first place. Dewart's rejection of reduplicative certainty is not a bypassing of (b), while his insistence on a (practical) "disbelief" is an attitude (equally practical!) to ensure that our faith as a state of consciousness not amount to what (again, practically) would be a Pelagianism of the intellect. In short, Dewart's "doubt" would affect the intellect only so that the *consciousness* of faith continue to defer to the mystery of revelation.

of contemporary understanding that is what (unconsciously, of course) it could easily come to. Or, this would be the kind of speculation easily affecting, at least for all practical purposes, the infinite transcendence of God. This, indeed, is precisely the reason why Reformation thinking has always rejected the analogy of being, and, indeed, in most cases, the very possibility of a "natural theology." Though there is no doubt at the bottom of this a basic dualism of God/man, or God/world, this is evidently not the only reason. Dewart's objection is otherwise somewhat different from this line of argument; his is rather that to attribute existence to God is to anthropomorphize him. He does not thereby claim that this would be an inevitable consequence of the Thomistic analogy of being, but rather, and more relevantly, that the contemporary notion of existence no longer suits the Scholastic one.

Dewart's alternative suggestion is not to think of God as "being" (in the verbal sense) at all. Whether that is necessarily a better proposal remains to be seen. Scholastically trained historians of philosophy might even feel some qualms when recognizing here a speculative move uncannily resembling one found in Plotinus, who refuses to predicate "being" of the "*hen*," the "One." But understandable though such objections would be, they would also be to misunderstand our author; first because his rejection of hellenistic categories more in general hardly make him a suspect in the matter of relying on gnostic dualism; second, because once a semantic proposal is made, it is obviously admissible to pursue it to its logical conclusion. And the reason for the semantic proposal is that the contemporary notion of existence is considerably more phenomenological than ontological. Dewart is not saying that God does not exist in the way the atheist would claim the same; he is saying that God is *beyond* existence, this term having the contemporary connotations it does. Whether the notion of existence should loom so large as it does in Dewart's

171

thinking remains to be seen; but the proposal is a serious one, and therefore a serious competitor to the traditional Scholastic notion bearing the same name.

But even this is not enough. Dewart is not satisfied with a terminological rejection alone. More positively, he wants to see as most vital and functional in modern Christian thinking the conception of the "presence" of God. He recognizes several advantages of this. First, he invokes Marcel's distinction between existence and presence, the first being an uninspiring ontological category, and the second implying personal relationship: I am present only if I am present *to someone;* second, by this conception of the presence of God in human history he avoids the dialectics of transcendence/immanence, which, though no doubt consistent within a certain system, is confusing rather than enlighting for *understanding.* The experience of the faith does not in any way stand to benefit by dialectic speculation of this kind. (In the full-length version of the present paper it is attempted to show that the notion of the "presence" of God as "present to us" is also utterly biblical, so much so that it perhaps constitutes the most comprehensive "inclusion" in the entire Bible.)

DEVELOPMENT, CONSCIOUSNESS, CONCEPTUALIZATION, AND CULTURE

The preceding was mainly about the distortions in Christian thinking for which the hellenic frame of reference has been largely responsible. A more positive line of thinking in the book under review, although likewise in confrontation with the hellenic problem of knowledge, is the elaboration of the notion of consciousness and its development. This is relevant seeing that (as noted before) in the opinion of the author the faith is a state of consciousness, rather than an intermediate set of truths, to be assented to if the believer is to approach God at all. Dogma of course could be taken in its more reflexive sense in which theology is a reflection on the faith rather than the faith itself, in the sense, therefore, that "dogma" might indicate a *corpus doctrinae*. However, even in that case it should be as closely related to faithful consciousness as possible, and Dewart seems to be using the notion of dogma rather in this sense of very close relatedness, more than in its comparatively "autonomous" sense of (professional) dogmatic theology. For all practical purposes, the development of dogma as discussed by Dewart might stand for development of the faith itself. Consequently, the essence of (faithful) consciousness is elaborated in Dewart's book.

Development, says the author, is of the essence of consciousness. Traditional Scholastic metaphysics has looked for the nature of human consciousness too much in its reduplicative nature, as different from the consciousness of animals. Scholasticism, otherwise, speaks of knowledge rather than of consciousness; man is not only a knower, but he also knows that he knows; it is therefore self-reflexive. In this manner, and phrasing it now in post-Scholastic terms, the essence of human consciousness has come to be seen in the *cogito* (recently, and most dualistically, in Sartre). However, though there is certainly such a thing as the heightening of consciousness, this only accidentally entails the possibility of self-reflexion. Indeed, that element is mostly dispensable, and always inessential. First, consciousness as reduplicative self-awareness is also found, although to a lesser degree, in animals, so that the difference between man and animals should not be looked for there in the first place. But, more importantly, the heightening of consciousness, which is the very rationale of its development, is intensification rather than self-reduplication. The intensification consists in a progressive differentiation of the self, the things of our world, and others.

Consciousness, moreover, is not the same as knowledge, this

being only one aspect of conciousness. If, however, the faith is a (God-given) state of consciousness, truth can be no longer the correspondence between the knower and the known. Admittedly, the act of faith has always been distinguished from other acts of knowledge, because of the difference of the respective "objects," but the underlying notion of truth has been essentially the same. In either case it has been considered to be immutable. In this too rationalistic conception of the faith development has been mainly understood as a better knowledge of things already known previously, because the acquisition of things previously unknown, an alternative possible in the sciences, is usually excluded from the faith since after the apostolic period there has been no new revelation; and in so far as development of dogma has been deemed possible at all, it has been understood mainly as an explicitation of the *depositum fidei.*

This position, however, overlooks the nature of human experience, of which consciousness is, as it were, the crystallization. Consciousness, then, is not a succession of mental states, but the function or activity by which the being of man himself emerges. It does not, that is, develop as an additional faculty to "being" (Scholasticism would speak of the intellect as an "accident," albeit a necessary one), or, it is not a perfection which it acquires supererogatorily. Since, then, development is of the very essence of consciousness, truth cannot be the adequation of the intellect to an object, but fidelity of consciousness to being. Precisely for that reason there is some truth in all knowledge, and there can be no such thing as an absolute falsehood, because an absolute falsehood would have no connection whatsoever with our experience, of which, it bears repeating, consciousness is the crystallization. This, of course, would be an untenable position in a conception where "judgments" are supposed to be the joining or separating of subject and predicate, to which, then, the order of reality supposedly gives or denies its fiat. This would be true only if knowledge were some external over-all faculty like the agent intellect of Averroës. This is not only not true of man (as Thomas well realized), but not even of God, because it would radically presuppose a "pre-established harmony." The Aristotelico-Thomistic notion of truth is therefore not only contrary to empirical fact, but it also leads to the impossible conclusion of "God's truth" as the yardstick of everything. The notion of stability of truth entailed in such a conception of God's truth leads to its annihilation. Rather than conformity, truth is fidelity. As Dewart words it (italics his): "*Conformity* is a relation towards another which is owing to another by reason of the other's nature. *Fidelity* is a relation towards another which one owes to oneself by reason of one's own nature. Conformity obliges from the outside. Fidelity, like nobility, obliges from the within." [11]

Dewart does not work out explicitly the remarkable parallel between his theory of truth and his notion of relative theism, but it is so striking that it is worth doing this here, if briefly. If absolute theism is the position inclined towards the belief that anything is apt to be God, the traditional notion of absolute truth is the theory that man can have an overall view of reality, if only in principle, analogous to the overall view of reality that God must have. Therefore, to the conception of relative theism as the only theism which is free from the dangers of idolatry, there corresponds the notion of relative truth which prevents man from tending to consider omniscience as at least remotely within his power, or supposedly the prerogative of metaphysical thinking. That such a conception of relative truth is *toto caelo* different from, and indeed incompatible with, what in Scholastic thinking is (rightly) rejected as "relativism" is clearer than daylight. "Relativism" enables a thinker to ignore truths previously

11. *The Future of Belief*, p. 96.

established, the conception of relative truth (different also, it should be noted, from "agnosticism" in the modern sense) leaves the way open for refinement not only in the way in which Scholasticism would accept this, but also in terms of integration in changed times and cultures.

When the author then proceeds to apply his conception of consciousness and its development to the development of dogma, two forms of this development come up: the one in the individual person (called ontogenetic development by Dewart), and the other in the history of mankind (the phylogenetic one). About the first there is no basic issue: that faith develops in the individual person has not, I think, ever been denied; the very gospels testify to this in the case of the apostles. The point, therefore, is to show that there is development phylogenetically. For it is upon this aspect that the development of dogma should be brought to bear. Dewart does not really show that there is development in that over-all sense; that is, though there is no doubt such a thing as change of consciousness and therefore also of the faith over the times, and also a growth in awareness of certain features of human existence not realized so adequately previously, yet this is not the same as to say that there is an *overall* growth. More concretely, is there really evidence that the twentieth century is more developed, more generally or in matters of the faith, than previous centuries in all respects? Is there no regression in human history possible, or stagnation, in so many respects that the gains with regard to a few features are not able to restore the picture of a development (for the better) in a more comprehensive sense? It is not clear if that is the basic claim made by the author, but if it is, it must be asked whether it has been proven. While much more could be said about this aspect, we shall now convey the gist of the structure of (phylogenetic) development (taken in whatever sense), as presented by Dewart.

Consciousness, Dewart argues, faithful consciousness not excepted, necessarily entails conceptualization. Indeed, that is what spells the differences between experience and consciousness. If for no other reason, this argues that the faith cannot be expected to adhere perennially to certain fixed formulas of dogma, unless they have been given living form in such conceptualizations. However, the latter is, as is now abundantly well known from the behavioral sciences, not a matter of abstraction of the potentially intelligible from the actually sensible (as Scholasticism would have it), but a matter of cultural form. The communicability of concepts has long been conceived of as due to two factors, (a) the possibility that several minds might abstract the same intelligible object, (b) the possibility of conventional agreement on signs to represent such abstractions. Hence, man's mind has been dichotomized not only into the intelligible and the sensible, but also into thought and language. All the results, however, of scientific research are there to show that, if we conceive of consciousness as experience having reached the level of conceptualization, neither of these dichotomies makes any sense. While culture and language are natural to man, no given culture or language is the natural culture or language of man. The development Dewart has in mind is not the same as what is called acculturation, however necessary this may otherwise be; for acculturation is adaptation and it does not reflect the concept of change, consisting in the ever progressing conceptualization of and our never ending dissatisfaction with the truth as presented to us at a certain moment, age, or stage. While this is true for consciousness not concerned with the faith, it is even more true for the faith, since that is concerned with the inevident. I should add here that Dewart argues at some length that his conception is entirely different from the type of modernism condemned in *Pascendi*. The arguments he adduces for this are so convincing that it is not necessary to attend to them here, and the reader may therefore be referred to Dewart's book for this particular issue.

177

DEWART'S MAIN INSPIRATION . . .

So far some of the basic ideas which lead the author in his theology, have been conveyed here in what is hopefully not too inadequate a manner. Some interesting consequences of these ideas follow for trinitarian theology and christology for today and we shall briefly mention them later. It seems now time for an assessment of the ideas developed so far, this time also confining ourselves to some major issues.

An extensive critique, indeed, would be faced with many problems. It would, for example, have to point out some inadequacies from the point of view of the history of philosophy. I will here merely mention three of them. First, it seems that Dewart's interpretation of Descartes is somewhat faulty, in that he attributes a logical quality to the inference implied in the *Cogito, ergo sum,* whereas according to Descartes himself the illation was a *direct* one, something pre-logical, therefore.[12] Second, Dewart repeats what histories of philosophy say about Averroës' hypostatization of the Aristotelian *nous poietikos;* however, it seems that careful reading of the third book of *Peri Psyches* leaves a distinct possibility open that Aristotle himself believed, in a return to Platonism surprising in such a late work, in such a *nous* of extraterrestrial status.[13] Third, Dewart claims that the thinking of Teilhard de Chardin was not primarily apologetic; however, this is a theological category, and in view of the fact that theologians who have written in great depth upon the French

12. See Wolfgaing Struve, "Ueber das *'ergo'* in Descartes' *ego cogito, ergo sum* und *sum, ergo Deus est,*" *Lexis* 2 (1951), pp. 239–62.

13. See F. J. C. J. Nuyens, S.J., *Ontwikkelingsomenten in de zielkunde van Aristoteles,* Nijmegen, 1939. Nuyens' work is a substantial improvement upon Werner Jaeger's famous *Aristoteles* (Berlin, 1923), especially, though not only, in the analysis of *Peri Psyches.*

paleontologist, de Lubac and Smulders,[14] distinctly claim apologetic status for Teilhard's thought, it seems that some substantiation on the part of Dewart would be needed for such an extraordinary claim.

More important, but also more elusive and therefore more difficult to assess, is Dewart's appraisal of hellenic thought, especially because he does not so much describe Greek thought in its own terms as the underlying frame of reference, for example, where he says that the Greeks considered being as necessary, or that the Parmenidean principle of being as convertible with intelligibility is the kind of thinking that foreshadowed, and inspired, the over-all preoccupation with matters epistemological in later Western thought. Claims like these are obviously different from the ones challenged in the preceding paragraph. True, also these characterizations of Greek thinking are not strictly proven by the author. On the other hand, there is a distinct convergence of evidence in that direction, and at least as a hypothesis it seems as sound as any of that magnitude that could be made. For example, and following such a claim into its historical aftermath, there is little doubt that the Thomistic dictum *anima est quodammodo omnia,* itself a literal translation of an Aristotelian quote, ultimately goes back to that Parmenidean principle. Similarly, it would take a ponderous monograph to prove that pessimism was

14. Henri de Lubac, S.J., *The Faith of Teilhard de Chardin,* London, 1965, esp. pp. 133 ff. P. Smulders, S.J., *The Vision of Teilhard de Chardin,* Glen Rock, 1964: Smulders points out that in the whole *oeuvre* of Teilhard the distinctly *non*-apologetic passages (mainly the ones that have laid themselves open to suspicion of unorthodoxy, as different from objections against Teilhard on the part of those who failed to understand the apologetic approach) are largely unrelated to his phenomenology, and very little representative of Teilhard's general method. Whether this can still be held after hitherto unedited material has become available, of course remains to be seen. See also Robert L. Faricy, S.J., "Teilhard de Chardin's Theology of Redemption," *Theological Studies* 27 (1966), pp. 553–79.

a distinct feature of Greek ideas, yet it is reasonable to expect that the diagnosis is basically accurate, and I am not sure that many Graecologists would want to question it. The underlying notion of necessity of being is manifested perhaps more clearly by the absence of any radical notion of contingency in Greek thinking, especially because the later act-potency doctrine in Aristotle is by no means a radical approach to the problem of contingency, but rather an attempt to deal with change, and, at greater depth, with the problem of the one and the many. As for the undercurrent of pessimism, apart from what might be said on this by students of Greek drama, or by those of the typically Greek conception of history as cyclic, in the act-potency doctrine alone it would be difficult not to recognize just a more down-to-earth and more empirical version of the Platonic depreciation of earthly reality. Closely related to this pessimism is the fatalism of Greek *ananke,* the demythologized descendant of the earlier *moira,* an all-pervading force so potent, and indeed so much of a law (presumably, it might be hypothesized, the ancestor of the Thomistic *lex naturalis*), that even Zeus was supposed not to interfere with it. While the *physis* of the *kosmos* was a closed system, the "morality" element (but, characteristically, a *blind* one) of the order in that *kosmos* was concretized in the latter's careful compartmentalization, every part having some deity or demon in charge of it, while it was imperative that no god meddle with a part not under his supervision. Even Zeus was not supposed to infringe upon this order, but only to enforce its implementation; and what we therefore have here is a (rather epiphenomenal) embryonic concept of a supreme being, blind, nameless, and not to be defied. The *ananke,* resp. *moira,* was blind precisely because the *kosmos* had the self-supporting characteristics that in later ontology would have to be called necessity.[15]

15. Cf. also F. M. Cornford, *From Religion to Philosophy: A Study in the Origins of Western Speculation,* New York, 1957.

So far Dewart's characterizations of hellenic thinking are to be taken entirely seriously. While I do not feel competent to say how far they are substantiated by specialistic research in Greek thinking, I would, however, call attention to the problem of *hellenistic* thought, in the sense of post-classical, as distinguished from the classical Greek period up to and including Aristotle, say, the *hellenic* period. The importance of this is not that Dewart should have taken into account refinements of the kind involved in the transition from hellenic to hellenistic thinking, but rather that Scholasticism cannot be traced back to (say) Aristotle directly. The connection is in many ways an indirect one.[16] This matter has not been deeply investigated in general, but, more seriously, Scholastic philosophers are, on the whole, entirely unaware of it. For example, the Thomistic notion of *substantia* is, from an ontological point of view, more different

16. For what follows I am especially indebted to the following publications of Johannes Lohmann: "M. Heidegger's 'ontologische' Differenz und die Sprache," *Lexis* 1 (1948), pp. 49–106; "Was ist und was will allgemeine Sprachwissenschaft?," *Lexis* 1 (1948), pp. 128–168; "Erik Wistrand, Ueber das Passivum (Besprechung)," *Lexis* 1 (1948), pp. 280–298; "Vom ursprunglichen Sinn der aristotelischen Syllogistik," *Lexis* 2 (1951), pp. 205–236; "Das Verhältnis des abendländischen Menschen zur Sprache (Bewusstein und unbewusste Form der Rede)," *Lexis* 3 (1953), pp. 5–49; " 'Sprache' und 'Zeit'," *Studium Generale* 8 (1955), pp. 562–567; " 'Wort' und 'Zahl', Eine geschichtliche Studie zu Begriff und Realität von 'Bedeutung'," *Zeitschrift für slavische Philologie* 25 (1956), pp. 151–158. For *substantia* and related terms I have derived material from C. W. M. Verhoeven, "Het woord *substantia*," Tijdschrift voor Philosophie 22 (1960), pp. 495–543. With Lohmann compare M. Heidegger, *Einführung in die Metaphysik*, Tübingen, 1958. For a more comprehensive discussion of the subject-object split incidental to Stoic philosophy as compared to classical Greek thinking see my *Some Relations Between Perception, Speech, and Thought*, Assen, 1963, esp. 77–80. With regard to all these publications, with the exception, it seems to me, of Verhoeven, some reservations have to be made.

from Aristotle's *ousia* than similar to it. Indeed, the fact that Thomas did not know Greek did not particularly predispose him to understand Greek thought adequately. While the meaning of Aristotle's *ousia* is quite adequately conveyed by the present-day English expression "concrete reality," the credentials of Thomas's *substantia* can be traced back no farther than Boethius. While *substantia* as the original rendering of Aristotle's *ousia* was still a denominative of the verb *substare* "to stand firm," "to stand rooted," for Boethius it was—gratuitously—a derivative of *stare sub* (i.e., *accidentibus*), which means a definitive deviation from the Aristotelian notion.[17]

Further research in line with Dewart's investigations would have to be continued by studying the later fate of Aristotelian concepts before they found their home in medieval Scholasticism. Our example of *substantia,* which we cannot now pursue any further, is obviously not just an arbitrary example. It is precisely this notion that functions in traditional Trinity tracts, its historical study is closely related to that of *essentia* and several other notions that have functioned in the hellenization of Christian dogma, like *hypostasis.* It is widely enough known that the christological disputes until Chalcedon were deeply frustrated by linguistic confusions.[18]

17. Indeed, within the Thomistic system itself *substantia* is a notion with heavy epistemological overtones, since it is defined as *unum per se; unum,* however, is defined in a double negation, i.e., as *indivisum in se* and *divisum ab omni alio.* Actually, the closest non-epistemological (or non-formal, if you will) approximation to *substantia* in the Thomistic system is *actus primus,* but that cannot be made to serve the systematic purposes of the notion of *substantia.*

18. See J. N. D. Kelly, *Early Christian Doctrines,* New York, 1959; while many of these confusions have been noted in specialistic studies of the history of the trinitarian and christological disputes, it seems that there is not yet available the kind of comprehensive monograph of hellenistic Greek (*koine*) analyzed contrastively with regard to classical Greek, as underlying, that is, the confusions that have inhibited a more harmonious consensus in the first few centuries of the Christian era.

The Greek philosophical tradition went into medieval Scholasticism through the hellenistic period into Latin. Quite many subtle differences between Aristotelian and Thomistic thinking should be explained by this tremendously complicated transition. In this virtually no research has been done so far. Heidegger's unparalleled intuition of the underlying forces of Western "foregetfulness of being" (*Seinsverguessenheit*) as compared to earliest Greek thinking has perhaps been the greatest contribution so far, but that philosopher's lack of philological detachment does not commend his efforts to the more sober-minded researchers; Johannes Lohmann pursued similar but more scholarly investigations in the now defunct journal *Lexis,* but it failed to elicit serious response from other scholars, also because they were understandably deterred by Lohmann's blind insistence on Western decadence as compared to classical Greek thinking from which in his view it had so ignominiously defected. Lohmann's principal thesis is that Stoic interference with classical Greek thought effectuated a subject-object split entirely absent in classical Greek philosophy. For purposes of brevity this difference might be worded as follows: while the "subject," or the self, is still a factor or *ordering* in classical Greek thought, later it becomes a factor of *disturbance;* there is a world of difference (in terms, that is, of the underlying frame of reference) between *lego* and *cogito, krisis* and *iudicium, energeia* and *actus, dynamis* and *potentia, physis* and *natura, aporia* and *dubium, toi onti* and *re vera;* the first in each of these pairs states the concept in terms of objectivity, equally applicable to "subjects" as to "objects" (but this of course is already a post-hellenic formulation), while the second in each pair is, say, "subjectivized"; *krisis,* for example, is just "separation," and not the judge's act of passing sentence as implied in *iudicium, energeia* is still reasonably close to what we now call "energy," an objective category therefore, while *actus* is what is done by *personal agent,* a subject; not, of course, explicitly, but by way of an underlying metaphor.

183

It is clear that in the hellenistic (in the sense of post-classical) period the *physis* no longer was the closed system, at one time still quite unproblematically including the human self. When the self jumped out of the objective *physis,* it of course acquired all the paraphernalia of transcendence, became the "judge" of truth in a manner which opened the way for God's truth in the absolute notion of truth as elaborated above. Is it not perhaps much more to Stoic thinking that we should trace the sophistication of epistemological issues, as so largely characterizing Western thought in the manner also meant by Dewart, rather than to the hellenic Parmenidean principle? Is there not much more of an unbroken line between the transcendental analyses of Kant, back through Descartes' "turn to the subject" (*die Wende zum Subject,* to use Husserl's characterization of Descartes' philosophy), back again to the Stoic separation of subject and object; and only a broken, and even somewhat discontinuous, line from modern Western obsession with epistemology, back to Parmenides? These are questions which a deeper analysis of Dewart's claims than can be attempted here would have to ask.

Comparable problems arise when we attend to Dewart's interpretation of medieval Scholasticism. The same difficulty arises here as above: the author is investigating the underlying Scholastic frame of reference rather than what Scholasticism explicitly claims. While this task is more rewarding, it is also more elusive. But for the same reason Dewart's attempts deserve all the more attention. For example, is it so undoubtedly clear that Thomas's problem was the clash between the Greek notion of necessity and his own theistic notion of the contingency of being? And if so, was it that which led him to the indeed basic claim of the real distinction between essence and existence? In terms of explicit thinking the way Thomas arrived at his real distinction was certainly different. He distinguished "being" (in its verbal meaning as *formalissimum quid,* where *"formalis"* meant "basic" or "fundamental") from the "beings" (in its nominal meaning); or, he made the distinction later to be phrased by Heidegger as the "ontological difference" (*ontologische Differenz*). Actually, objectivity obliges us to point out to Dewart that Thomas's distinction was not between *essentia* and *existentia,* but between *essentia* and *esse.* This is, of course, not denied by the author, since he is concerned rather with implicit assumptions. This makes Dewart's interpretation hard to assess.[19]

. . . AND FOLLOWING IT UP

It seems a safe claim that all Western metaphysics derives from hellenic thinking. All the major lines of thought in the Occident can be traced back along broken and quite frequently along unbroken lines, to the philosophy that began with the Pre-Socratics; sharply divergent philosophies in the West like the thought of Nietzsche still rely on hellenic culture, even though the Dionysian cult is there confronted with and preferred

19. It seems that in Thomas's earlier work *esse* is still seen as what *"accidit qualitati"* than as what *"accidit essentiae." Esse* is then increasingly regarded as *perfection,* suiting a frame of reference of participation. This is a somewhat simplified view of what in fact is a rather complicated development in the works of St. Thomas (complicated also by unsettled issues concerning the chronology of these works), for the details of which I am indebted to class notes of a course by M. Marlet, S.J., now at Innsbruck. See Chapter VI of his *Grundlinien der kalvinistischen "Philosophie der Gesetzesidee" als christlicher Transzendentalphilosophie,* Munich, 1954, pp. 111–25. Even though Dewart outlines the *underlying* frame of reference rather than the *explicit* systematic treatment on the part of Thomas, thus making him comparatively immune against a critique relying *directly* on texts from Thomas's works, yet Dewart's terminology must be called unfortunate. On the other hand, Suarezian Scholasticism has always worked with *existentia* rather than with *esse.*

to the Socratic developments. Iconoclasts, like Freud or the Vienna Circle, are ultimately as much indebted to the beginnings of Ionia. It seems therefore a good question, whether there could be a metaphysics at all independent of those sources. Obviously, one might here point to Oriental metaphysics, as in Indian philosophies. But those are religiously inspired; for that matter, the metaphysics of the West is also of distinctly religious origin. Metaphysics as we know it is the secularization of religious thought, or the demythologizing process from, to take a familiar pair of concepts, *mythos* to *logos*.[20] As Auguste Comte already observed, metaphysics is a transition from theology to science, when taken in its developmental aspect.[21] It must therefore be asked if metaphysics has a value independent of this transitional function. Dewart does not ask this question, although occasionally he comes quite close to doing so.

The question must be asked for many reasons, and I shall review some of those reasons to begin with. First, metaphysics is deeply mistrusted nowadays; in fact, it is generally rejected, either in the name of science, or in the name of philosophies which claim to replace the task at one time fulfilled by metaphysics, as in certain types of phenomenology and in many contempo-

20. See W. Nestle, *Vom Mythos zum Logos*, Stuttgart, 1940. There are some worthwhile linguistic and cultural studies on the transition from the mythic to the philosophic world view, but they do not seem to have influenced philosophical studies to any notable degree. A good specimen is Gustav Mensching's "Religionswissenschaft und Sprachwissenschaft," *Lexis* 3 (1953), pp. 240–244. The only notable exception to philosophical negligence of this topic in recent times is Ernst Cassirer, *The Philosophy of Symbolic Forms*, vol. I, *Language*, New Haven, 1953, and vol. II, *Mythical Thought*, New Haven, 1955; but Cassirer was heavily Kantian, although with a refreshing admixture of phenomenology. For a briefer and less technical exposition see his *An Essay on Man*, New York, 1953.

21. See Henri de Lubac, *The Drama of Atheist Humanism*, New York, 1963, pp. 79 ff.

rary non-traditional philosophies largely concerned with logic, semantics, the analysis of language, philosophy of science, criteriologies. Many philosophers consider metaphysics to be a crypto-theology. A more general disapproval is based upon the claim that metaphysical statements cannot be subject to confirmation (empirically or otherwise) or disconfirmation. Metaphysics, in short, and revealingly, is nowadays only believed in by those having religious interests in one form or another. Exceptions to this rule are in many cases only apparent: Heidegger, for example, has claimed to be a phenomenologist rather than a metaphysician (though he does use the term "metaphysics"), or, for that matter, an existentialist. Hartshorne does consider himself a metaphysician, but on closer inspection his aims turn out to be an overall organization of thinking and therefore a criteriology rather than metaphysics.[22]

Second, the status and function of the metaphysical component of Christian (both Protestant and Catholic) dogmatic theology is extremely unclear, as deeply distrusted as in the cases cited above, and frequently felt to be incompatible with the organization of biblical themes (biblical theology as different from exegesis). The *ratio theologica* of the theses of traditional dogmatic tracts is usually somewhat out of tune with the rest of the thesis under consideration.

Third, metaphysics is often implicit in a manner not generally recognized as such. Thus Bultmann's definition of myth, when compared with the sophistication of his expert knowledge of Scripture strikes one as comparatively naïve, and certainly unproven.

Fourth, it seems almost impossible to find an objective appraisal of metaphysics as a type of philosophy. Most modern philosophers opposing it are only sketchily familiar with it; their

22. See, for example, "Some Reflections on Metaphysics and Language," *Foundations of Language* (1966), pp. 2, 20–32.

187

intuition concerning the nature of metaphysics may, for all we know, be right, but it is generally not *shown* to be. Metaphysicians themselves are not very well disposed to foundational appraisal of their avocation; indeed, their lack of familiarity with modern philosophy comes quite close to the lack of interest on the part of modern philosophers in metaphysics. Characteristically, those metaphysicians drawing upon contemporary philosophy are largely interested in genres still basically metaphysical, especially the existentialists. Where the affinity with traditional metaphysics is more remote, as in many types of phenomenology, metaphysicians will use that trend as a beginning, in the sense that they consider phenomenology as at a certain stage superseded; lacking, as it is sometimes claimed, in depth.

Studies in the nature of metaphysics are comparatively rare. Georges Gusdorf has pointed out that "myth" is typical not only of primitive ways of thinking, but also (versus Lévi-Bruhl) of sophisticated ways of thinking like metaphysics.[23] The now defunct linguistic analysis school of Cambridge ("therapeutic" analysis, taking up one line of Wittgenstein's inspiration) claimed that though metaphysics is "meaningless" it yet serves a purpose, showing that metaphysical questions are unanswerable, and therefore freeing the questioner from a "problem," in a manner analogous to the way emotional problems are solved by psychoanalysis. Metaphysics, in this conception, is "important nonsense."[24]

It may be in order to make entirely clear that it is *not* here maintained that dogmatic theology can ever legitimately be a metaphysics. The latter is philosophy and cannot deal with the *mysteria stricte dicta.* I am here referring to a metaphysical

23. Georges Gusdorf, *Mythe et métaphysique,* Paris, 1953.
24. This expression is found in Wittgenstein. See John Wisdom, *Other Minds,* Oxford, 1952. On the whole of "therapeutic analysis" see Maxwell John Charlesworth, *Philosophy and Linguistic Analysis,* Pittsburgh, 1961, pp. 150–167.

framework rather than metaphysics; or, certain features of metaphysical methodology, or certain metaphysical presuppositions are relevant to the kind of dogmatic theology under discussion. When in what follows I speak, for the sake of brevity, of "metaphysical" or "metaphysicalized" theology, this stipulation should be constantly borne in mind.

A good example, then, is one elaborated by Dewart. He attacks the kind of theology which starts out (as Thomas does) from the theodicy God, then to proceed to a theology of the three Persons. As these three Persons exist "in" that one God, the theodicy approach is either supposed, or made into the framework for Trinitarian theology, and quite probably both. The New Testament, however, does not start out from the one God, not even from the Old Testament conception of Yahweh (which would otherwise be quite unlike the theodicy approach), but it starts out from the three Persons.

The most over-all characterization in more concrete terms of this metaphysicalized theology is found when we recognize how creation and elevation are related to one another. In this theology creation is made to be the framework of elevation, because creation is a subject supposedly accessible to philosophy, while elevation is not. Thus creation is presupposed, and on the basis of that elevation is brought in in a manner that *might* and *does* make it look like something additional, or even contingent. Once created, the argument goes, man sinned; then God remedied man's plight by the Incarnation. The point of course is that God need not have done so; this seems implied in the claim that God redeemed man "freely." This freedom of God is determined in terms of a *possibilia* theology. The Franciscan school thought that God would have become incarnate anyway, but now that man had sinned, its purpose became one of redemption. The theology of the motive of the Incarnation has been long and rather fruitlessly discussed; the background was of course an anthropomorphized conception of God's salvific Providence.

189

Whatever the opinion, creation is presupposed before redemption.[25] In Trinitarian theology this framework comes out in the distinction between the *processiones* and the *missiones*. If the two were not distinct, it is felt, it would seem as if the former could not exist without the latter. And that again would jeopardize the notion of the freedom of God.

In Holy Scripture the perspective is precisely the reverse: the Covenant is the perspective within which creation is viewed.[26] Yahweh the creator is in the first place the God of the Covenant. In the New Testament the Incarnation is not an afterthought with regard to creation: everything has been created in Christ, that is, in the Word *incarnate*. Thus in Colossians 1, 15–17. The Logos of the Prologue to the Gospel of John is likewise the Logos having become flesh. The Bible has no qualms about what has come to be called the "problem" of the preexistence of Christ.[27] Malmberg quotes a theologian's question what would happen if the human nature of Christ were to be

25. On the whole question of the "motive" of redemption see the excellent brief survey and commentary in Chapter I of F. Malmberg's *Ueber den Gottmenschen*, Freiburg, 1960.

26. Scripture scholars are so aware of this that it is surprising mention of this in dogmatic theology is so rare. See P. De Haes, *De schepping als heilsmysterie*, Tielt, 1962; Th. Mouiren, *La création*, Paris, 1962; H. Renckens, *Israel's Concept of the Beginning: The Theology of Genesis I–III*, New York, 1964; the latter book is a Scripture study which, though relying on exegetical material, is more geared to biblical theology, with comments even of a dogmatic nature.

27. In the perspective of Christ's "pre-existence" a text like Genesis 1, 27 ("in His likeness and image") takes on profound dimensions. For the concrete Jewish mentality, "in His likeness and image" could not mean anything else but "as His son;" in fact, the same phrase is used for Adam begetting Seth, Gen. 5, 3. It must have been this theme that was picked up by Luke, 3, 38b. The profound N.T. dimension of the Genesis text is seriously damaged by the traditional Thomistic interpretation of creation as one (though unique) instance of *agere simile sibi:* it reduces sonship to a depersonalized ontological similarity.

annihilated. The presupposition is that what is created by God can also be annihilated by him. Malmberg first states that the question is illegitimate, as it belongs to a *possibilia* theology; he goes on to say, once it is asked, the answer should be that in that case there would be *nothing left whatsoever of creation*.[28]

Metaphysical dogmatic theology generally overlooks a truth forcibly brought home frequently by Karl Barth, i.e., that the way God reveals himself is exclusively in the manner of what God is and means *for us*, not what he is *in himself*. It is indubitable that this point has been overemphasized by Barth, a feature which Bonhoeffer came to call Barth's "revelational positivism." The point is that, in the eschatological form of revelation in the New Testament, God has revealed himself in Jesus Christ *completely*. To think that we know the Father *partly* in Christ is ultimately a wrong-headed view of the human nature of Christ; in Christ the *plenitude* of God resides; while in traditional Trinitarian theology, the one of the *processiones* is (supposedly) distinct from the *missiones*, this would be unconditionally true only of the Word-not-incarnate. But the Word incarnate is not less the Son of the Father. Therefore we know God in Christ. Or, in the words of Rahner and in Trinitarian terms, the *processiones* are *completely* contained in the *missiones*,[29] and therefore in the Logos.

In this manner the mystery of elevation, or redemption, becomes the framework in which creation is viewed. It is the attitude of the Bible. It differs from the opposite viewpoint in that it is not apologetic; it may leave room for all sorts of doubts which are *practically* bound up with the inevidence or obscurity of the faith. It does not rest upon a philosophy which, in the well-known and humorous aphorism, whether it was used in conscious or unconscious self-derision, is *"de omni re scibili et de*

28. Malmberg, *op. cit.,* p. 93.
29. Karl Rahner, *Theological Investigations,* vol. I, Baltimore and Dublin, 1965, p. 148.

191

quibusdam aliis." The metaphysicalized type of dogmatic theology in the last analysis claims to know too much. In revelation God intimates to man that He, God, loves man. Then why would man even begin to ask why?

Precisely because metaphysical theology is basically apologetic, it is not obviously wrong-headed. It may well have fulfilled a useful apologetic function in earlier stages of the development of dogma. If it no longer does, that is not so much because apologetics has become superseded. Also Teilhard de Chardin is apologetic; but one does not have to believe in evolution first before believing in Christ.[30] Likewise one does not have to believe in metaphysics if one is to have faith. At one time it may have been useful to show philosophers, all of them metaphysicians, that the faith, far from being incompatible with philosophical knowledge, actually substantiates it; as it is useful now for scientists to see that there is a harmonious unity between the theory of evolution and the Christian faith. The difference is that a theory like that of evolution is in the heart of these times, while metaphysics is not. We therefore should abandon the metaphysical attitude.

The perils of metaphysical theology are by no means only relevant for Catholic theology, but also for Reformation thinking. Let an example be the rather notorious one of the Easter faith, as in the view of several theologians of Bultmannian inspiration. I will now sidestep the issue whether a consistent Bultmannian approach would claim that Christ was never resurrected.[31] However, this is often what is being claimed or at least suggested.[32] Roman Catholic belief, on the contrary, would hold

30. P. Smulders, *op. cit.*, Chapter VI.

31. See on this R. Bultmann *et al.*, *Kerygma and Myth*, New York, 1961 (German original 1948), pp. 38–43.

32. See P. Van Buren, *The Secular Meaning of the Gospel*, New York, 1963, *passim*.

that the Resurrection was indeed a revitalization of the dead body of Jesus Christ. I do not now claim that the issue, theologically speaking, could be decided completely by removing the underlying metaphysical assumptions of both positions. But it would certainly help to begin there. First, if the issue is posited in terms of the two alternatives indicated here, it overlooks the biblical view of the Resurrection, which is not only that Christ stood up from the tomb, but also, and *primarily,* that he was exalted at the right hand of God. The glorification was a divinization, worded as it was in the earliest of all creeds "Jesus is the Lord." As for particulars, the Resurrection narratives in the gospels exhibit various features not found in the narratives of Christ's public ministry. First, the fact of the Resurrection itself is not narrated, only that of the empty tomb. Second, Christ appeared to no one but believers. Third, even those who had known Him for years, frequently did not recognize Him. Fourth, the risen Jesus did things not recorded of his public ministry, like walking through closed doors, or disappearing. All this is enough to make us conclude (a) that his bodily presence is clearly and frequently attested; (b) that his presence is not for unbelievers; (c) that his bodily presence is not the same as before his death. To conclude from there to an "Easter faith" which amounts to no more than the emergence of an awareness of what Christ did and said during his public ministry, on the part of the apostles, is to metaphysicalize the Easter event as much as happens when the main emphasis is on the revitalization of the body. It is also typical of the metaphysical attitude to feel urged to choose between the one and the other. In the one case, to claim that a miracle is possible is as biased as to say that it is not. The bias is in the naïve conception of a miracle as (say) a violation of the "closed" system of the laws of nature, more than in the affirmation or denial of its possibility, which after all, are consequent upon that conception of the miracle. That conception, in its turn, is again deplorably out of tune with the biblical notion of the *dynamis,* the power of God, or *semeion,* a "sign" of eschatological import. For the Bible God is not a magician, and what has come to be called a "miracle" is, in the biblical conception, an event of extraordinary significance for the faith and/or the consummation, while it is also frequently an instance of the struggle between good and evil (as when Jesus "rebuked" the storm).

The secular meaning of the gospel, to use a phrase that is the title of a recent book,[33] is not the distortion of the dispensation of grace into a view of nature supposedly modern but ultimately of incredible *naïveté* and of a distinctly anachronistic metaphysical dogmatism. There are very few facts, whether theological, philosophical, or scientific ones, that cannot be made to clash with assumptions which seem to come natural once they are summoned up. To make the clash unavoidable does not always serve the theological interests of the point at issue. Granted, we should eliminate a notion of miracle which is unbiblical, based upon a completely "closed" view of "nature" (such a "closed" view, incidentally, is *not* modern and in straight contradiction with, say, prevailing notions in the philosophy of science), and making of God a divine magician who at one time, but not in modern times, showed that he can do it if he wants to. But the solution to this is obviously not to suggest that he can*not* do it if he wants to. *Both* conceptions are consequences of an absolute, and therefore *potentially* idolatrous, theism. Since an absolute theism inevitably drags down the mystery of God to mundane proportions, it is no wonder that the view of this mundane reality is equally absolute. Also this view is—and at this point we should almost expect it—unbiblical. For example, when that major event of Old Testament history of salvation, the liberation of the Hebrews from Egypt, came to be described, in the later versions, as a "miraculous" event, as compared to the earlier accounts, in which the

33. P. Van Buren, *op. cit.*

194

Red Sea fell dry rather as a "natural" phenomenon, the sacred authors were not changing their minds in favor of a theology of the miracle; all they did was to bring out more clearly the divine dimensions of Yahweh's fidelity to his people. This is not so much myth as a mythologization, a thing useful to remember in view of Cox's claim that the bible itself favors demythologization and secularization.[34] The Bible simply does both. It therefore cannot be invoked to support a notion of secularization which in actual fact is a naive allegiance to an outmoded view of nature of a basically metaphysical signature. The danger of metaphysics is that we want to know too much, and the inevitable consequence is that we end up by knowing too little.

In short: a "metaphysical" dogmatic theology may at one time have served apologetic purposes. It seems a safe claim that it no longer does. It should therefore be abandoned as soon as possible. Considered now not so much from a systematic but psychological point of view, the reason for still adhering to a metaphysicalized theology seems to be that it supposedly enhances the *certainty* of the faith by providing an over-all view of reality in which the mysteries of the faith are shown to fit. However, far from enhancing that certainly, all it accomplishes is more *clarity*. Clarity, however, is not the same as certainty. If this is already so in the philosophy and the sciences, how much more in faith, since that is inevident and obscure. To mistake clarity for certainty is, in the words of Dewart, to mistake *reduplicative* certainty for an essential feature of human consciousness. While the believer should have *concern* for the truth of what he believes, he should beware of expressing this concern in a way which makes him rely on the faith rather than on God. Therefore, a metaphysicalized dogmatic theology is, psychologically speaking, quite easily a form of crypto-Pelagianism, and an intrusion into the numinous.

34. Harvey Cox, *The Secular City*, New York, 1965, pp. 17–37.

Objectively speaking, it is a proud theology. But how can a proud theology be a reflection upon a humble faith? Like all pride, it is ultimately based on fear, and cognate to magic. Theology should have at least a remote analogy to the *disciplina arcana* in a Church when it was still young.

7.

The Challenge of Dehellenization

R. C. HINNERS

THE FUTURE OF BELIEF attempts "to sketch an approach to . . . the problem of integrating Christian thiestic belief with the everyday experience of contemporary man" (p. 7). This project is founded on the positive assumption that "contemporary experience should be understood as the mode of consciousness which mankind . . . has reached as a result of its historical and evolutionary development" (p. 9). The assumption is crucial since there are other "radical Christians" who believe "that the modern world needs to be vomited out of history." [1] For them Dewart's whole undertaking is "sheer reaction" since "it fails utterly to grasp the absolute liberty that the radical Christian senses." For him, the secular world "cannot determine my future and I owe it not the slightest allegiance." [2] I will try to show that this sort of disagreement, though absolutely crucial, need not and ought not,

1. F. Wilhelmsen, "Leslie Dewart: Heretic or Hellene?" *Triumph* (1967).
2. *Ibid.*

197

as Wilhelmsen claims it must, be a disagreement with which Christians must be content to "simply exchange testimonies and let the chips fall where they may."

Much of *The Future of Belief* is devoted to the negative task of showing how hellenized Christian theism, although quite appropriate for its time, is now "underdeveloped" for a "world come of age." This contention can and is being disputed. Thomists can point out that Dewart's criticisms of Thomism are only justified in the case of certain degenerate and outmoded interpretations of Aquinas but are not applicable to "the insights of the recent critical generation of Thomists." [3] At best Dewart then appears to be carrying out "a rearguard skirmish, an intramural service" and "he does not notice either those who have preceded him in this task or those who outdistance him." [4]

It is quite possible that such criticisms (which are becoming all too frequent) may succeed in dragging *The Future of Belief* into the current orbit of Catholic theological and philosophical scholarship and then in castigating the book because it fails to meet the standards and methods of a Rahner or a Lonergan. But I believe that this would be to miss the main point of Dewart's proposal, "the integration of Christian belief with the everyday experience of contemporary man." The main point is not whether or even how Christians once accomplished this integration, but rather the necessity that we do so today. (And as Dewart rightly insists, we cannot do it for today unless we project a future of belief for tomorrow.) The author proposes that the adequacy or truth of Christian conceptualizations be tested by the requirements of our given situation (p. 110), rather than merely by their coherence and consistency with traditional concepts. In short, if one wishes to defend the value of the work of other

3. M. Novak, "Belief and Mr. Dewart," *Commonweal* (February 3, 1967).

4. *Ibid.*

Christians against Dewart's critique of a hellenized Christian theism, then in all fairness to his proposal we should do so within the framework of his non-hellenic concept of truth as an historically specific and human self-achievement. Of course, one can reject such a "situational and relative" sense of truth and insist on a metaphysical standard of truth. But what is at issue here (and it is beautifully and dramatically represented by Wilhelmsen) is whether or not Christianity *must* be conceived metaphysically.

Dewart would probably agree that our "trouble these days is that we continue to think, over-rationalistically, that the main task is to get the Bible straight and then apply it or to get the Pope to say the right thing and then get everybody to live up to it, or to re-think the philosophical problems of God and then start talking a new theistic language." [5] But to stop being overly rationalistic is to practice and so also to project and conceive the sort of non-metaphysical sense of truth which Dewart proposes in appraising his position and those of others. On the other hand, to conceptualize one's nausea and rejection of contemporary experience is to insist that truth in the final analysis is metaphysical and even *a priori* and rationalistic. But if we really are being "overly rationalistic" then we would do well to conceptualize our rejection of contemporary experience *as a sickness,* a human sickness as well as a Manichaean disease which has for too long plagued Christian faith.

Yet it is not so simple once one begins to carry out Dewart's proposal. Though God is indeed present to us in our new life of absolute freedom and self-creation, he is also "inevident" and transcendent: "the problem for Christian philosophy is to explore that reality and . . . to try to understand the meaning of God's simultaneous presence and absence" (p. 184). The project of integrating Christian theism with contemporary experience is here confronted with a profound problem, a problem which the

5. Daniel Callahan, *Commonweal* (March 3, 1967).

author seems to recognize but never develops. If the Incarnation and redemption are a vocation for man "to imitate God through his (man's) free decision to define himself in a conscious existence," [6] then this new life will involve a transcendence of the old as well as the immanent presence of God to this new life of freedom. To be sure, this new life is not a substitute for the old: if it were then Wilhelmsen would be correct without qualification and man's secular project of history-making would be supplanted by an absolutely transcendent and ahistorical dimension of faith which would owe no allegiance to any secular project of the old man. In failing to develop the eschatological dimension of faith except negatively as dehellenization, Dewart ends up overstressing the immanence of God "in the mutual presence of God and man in the *conscious* creation of the world" (p. 195). What seems to be omitted in Dewart's account of faith is a further development of just *what* the Christian is conscious of in this creation. Surely it is *not only* the world. What seems to be omitted in Wilhelmsen's critique of Dewart is that Christian theism is not, as Dewart would put it, an absolute but a relative theism. "A theology of the future transcends this world or it is nothing," Wilhelmsen insists. But we would add that a theology of the future which is *only* a transcendence of this world is equally nothing unless of course it be replaced with a metaphysics which would idealize a sick hatred of the world.

If as Dewart points out (but does not develop) the new life is not a substitute for the old, then the vocation of the new life of freedom must be heard and responded to in the course of and in the midst of the projects and valuations of our old life. But this does not mean that the Christian should demonically identify his old secular, all-too-human project with that of the absolute freedom of his new life to which he is called, nor does it mean that

6. Dewart, "God and the Supernatural," *Commonweal* (February 10, 1967).

one must give up and become nauseated over one's old being. Rather, the vocation of the new life means that the projects which one finds oneself already engaged in are now transcended by a new "commitment of oneself, to a certain projected existence" (p. 59).

To do so, however, entails not only a theological understanding of the future of one's faith with respect to its source or the word of God, but also a critical stock taking of our current secular projects to become conscious that they are secular and so limited, finite, historical and our own. This becoming-conscious of the finiteness and mortality of our own secular projects, the recognition that our contingent being is yet *to be* made, and therefore to be made by us, all involve a critical reflection upon what we have been believing in as men. This reflection is then a metaphysical inquiry, not because it is *a priori* in its rejection of contemporary experience but, on the contrary, because it is a discovery of our contingency and of our freedom which is dreadful because it is so absolute. In our secular projects, indeed in our project of secularity itself, we discover then the transcendent presence of God negatively as the possibility of man's absenting or negating himself by allowing the utter failure of history. It is all very well to say that God will not let man destroy himself and his world if only "one has faith." But having faith is not an empty, negative transcendence any more than it is identifiable with historically immanent projects of the secular or the technological freedom of man. To be conscious and to take care that the two are *not integrated*—to assure that our faith is not demonic —is an essential aspect of Christian faith. To articulate this difference between our secular projects and our faith project must be done from within our secular projects metaphysically. The predominant project of hellenic man was hellenic speculative reason while the predominant project of contemporary man has become a rational but technological self-making of himself and

201

his world. To articulate the finiteness and contingency of these projects can be understood as a metaphysical ontology in that it uncovers, however negatively, the transcendence of God.

In short, I do not see how the future of theism can be developed only in terms of a phenomenological-ontological articulation of God's immanence in the Christian experience of faith (Dewart). Nor, on the other hand, do I think it can any longer be assumed to be already sufficiently developed in any hellenic metaphysics without leading us even further astray from our contemporary secular world. Rather, Dewart's provocative proposal of developing a future of Christian faith through a conscious dehellenization of dogma will, it seems to me, require that we also develop a new unhellenic critical awareness of how God transcends without destroying our all-too-human secular undertakings.

The originality and depth of Dewart's proposal is precisely that it would go beyond the current way of doing Catholic theology and philosophy, in that it would involve a highly critical reflection upon the roots of *philosophia* in relation to contemporary experience. If one finds the moral theology of Aquinas hedonistic, that should lead us not only to work out a better moral theology but also to examine what sounds like hedonism today to find out why it was not hedonism for St. Thomas. And just because it was not hedonism for Aquinas is hardly any reason for retaining a position which sounds hedonistic today, just as it would be equally absurd to reject our own comtemporary concepts and experiences in an attempt to get back to the thirteenth century so Thomism will not sound hedonistic any more. On the other hand, to urge interpretations of the moral philosophy and theology of Aquinas which would make his position "appropriate for our time" could of course be done: that would add one more member to the long line of the "successors" of St. Thomas, stretching from Suarez, John of St. Thomas, and Cajetan down to Maritain, Gilson, Maréchal, Rahner, Loner-gan, Coreth and Metz. Many of these "successors" may now appear "degenerate" and to have had their day, but do not all still remain 'true' because the principles, method or basic concepts of their work are the eternal truths of Thomism? To call some of them "degenerate" is merely to point out that others are up-to-date and I believe it is not difficult to draw the unhappy conclusion from this notion of Thomism that even a Rahner or a von Balthasar will soon be numbered among the "degenerate successors" of St. Thomas. Subtle, twisting and sophisticated up-to-date interpretations of Thomism are not only of dubious value as historical scholarship, but more importantly a problem such as hedonism (I think Dewart is right) is rooted in the hellenist metaphysics and ethics of Aquinas: no modernizing of Aquinas can resolve that problem adequately because it stems from a Thomist philosophy which is hellenic in principle (pp. 33–4).

As long as Catholic theology, and especially philosophy, per-sists in attempting more or less successfully to account for and appropriate contemporary concepts and experiences by fitting them into a fundamentally hellenist and even Thomist mold, then the future of theism is indeed bleak in that it will become increasingly irrelevant. Such a method is fundamentally the same defensive strategy as Tridentine theology and if it continues it will mean that Catholic theology will not only stay behind the scientific, technological and social projects of contemporary man but will likely fall even further behind them. This is in no way to disparage the work of such men as Rahner, Metz and von Baltha-sar; it is only to point out that their contributions have been as great as they have been despite their Thomism not because of it. Nor is it to suggest that they should have undertaken some sort of radical and explicit dehellenization as an essential part of their philosophical or theological method since it is highly unlikely that they would have been heard or understood had they done so.

Dewart has pointed out in more than one place (specifically in his references to the work of Rahner) how the significance of such work is to have penetrated behind hellenist categories. If dehellenization were now to be assumed *explicitly and consciously,* would not the renewal of Catholic theology and philosophy be still further accelerated and invigorated?

The need to do so is I think very great but so also are the problems. To place a taboo on all hellenic concepts would be an unwarranted and *a priori* restriction on the theologian's choice of concepts for his formulations. Moreover, if one were to set about dehellenizing dogma, and especially our hellenic concepts of God, dogma and the whole tradition of Catholic theology would become almost if not totally unrecognizable. Not only would this be something of a traumatic experience by forcing us to go too rapidly from childhood to adulthood; it would raise profound difficulties for any theological method which sees its function primarily as one of integration and synthesis of the past rather than as projective and futural. This former way of theologizing is fundamentally retrospective towards the primitive sources of revelation so that the future of faith would (supposedly) become explicit by integrating and interpreting the implicit totality contained in its process of being handed down from past to present. (Cf. von Balthasar, *Herrlichkeit* III, 1, p. 20.) Dehellenization, on the other hand, seems to be fundamentally a projection of a future of belief which is thrown back critically upon its past in order then to draw its concepts from an authentic present. (Cf. Heidegger, *Being and Time,* Sect. 74.) Theologizing as a retrospective and re-collecting synthesis and integration seems then to be incompatible with a "speculative" projection of a future of belief founded upon a disintegration with the past (hellenized) conceptualizations of faith. On the other hand, since Christian faith is fundamentally prospective, eschatological and futural (for Christian faith requires doing and not merely understanding), then it would seem that dehellenization must somehow become an essential part of a Christian's theologizing as well as of his philosophizing.

Now there is good reason to suspect that dehellenization may also be, if not primarily, a way of philosophizing which would be particularly relevant for a theology concerned with the future of belief. If this dis-integration and dehellenization were carried out adequately beforehand as a philosophical method, could it not provide the new concepts necessary for a positive theological conceptualization of faith? Dehellenizing would then be not so much philosophizing with a hammer, or a cautery, as it would an understanding and subversion of our inhibited concepts so that we could become explicitly conscious of them as myths or beliefs. This after all has been precisely the contribution of contemporary analyses of our tradition of *philosophia*. The expressions "dehellenization" and "demythologization" would then be not so negative as they sound: they are just ways of showing how certain inherited concepts are only myths or are only hellenic (and not eternally true) concepts. In this way they are not destroyed but their status is altered and we are freer to surpass them. One should indeed become critical of concepts and formulations accepted unconsciously from tradition: *ratio* should be applied to *auctoritas*. But we have yet to realize that the *ratio* of the tradition of *philosophia* has been functioning as the *auctoritas* of today especially in matters moral and theological. Consequently, we should be applying the critical techniques of today (analysis, dialectic, phenomenology) to the very principles and method of a *"ratio"* which has become today an *auctoritas*. If I am correct that this is what Dewart is proposing, then he is only advocating a synthesis of contemporary philosophical efforts which would in turn be integrated into the enterprise of Christian theology rather than any rationalizing of *philosophia* by clothing it in modern dress.

205

Then, for example, instead of calling the "certitude" of faith "pre-scientific" we could rather speak of the existential commitment of faith in a doing with its consequent tendency to be prospective or speculative and so dehellenizing in order to surpass its past conceptualizations. Dewart sees the conceptualizations of faith, i.e., its the-*ism,* to be relative and conditioned (p. 66)—relative to what we believe in (God) and so discriminating and self-critical of our conceptualizations of both what faith is and of "*which* God we believe in" (p. 68). Assuredly, Dewart's way of stating the case *is not* compatible with a faith which is from the start and so fundamentally an act of intellectual assent (p. 64). Dewart would stress that the *auditus fidei* is more fundamentally an "existential response." That would mean that theology is one aspect, albeit an essential part, of that response, namely, that aspect of existential faith which is "self-critical" and also speculative or concerned with the future of belief. In short, I would want to suggest that the hellenist notion of faith as some sort of intellectual ("although pre-scientific") act covers up the existential root of theology, in much the same way as Plato and Aristotle covered up the existential roots of the Socratic speculative faith of *philo-sophia* and probably for very much the same cultural-historical reasons.

Dewart's conception of theologizing as fundamentally prospective and critically retrospective (dehellenizing) thus involves profound revision of our philosophical understanding of knowledge so that truth becomes essentially situational or historically culturally specific (p. 110). Unless the negative term "dehellenization" is understood quite positively within this unhellenic concept of truth, then one might wrongly suppose, as Dr. Anderson appears to do, that Dewart is claiming, "Scholasticism Must Go." But dehellenization is no more a "cleansing of the stables of Greek ideas" than it is a "cauterizing" of them. Nor is "Greek metaphysics disposable in that a system is disposable":

206

indeed, I am unable to discover any passage in *The Future of Belief* in which the author claims that it is. Nor can I discover anywhere in this book, "the mythical supposition of a common 'Greek metaphysical tradition' . . . *in the sense of the passing on of a notionally uniform body of knowledge*" (italics mine). What Dewart not only "has in mind" but *does say* (pp. 45n, 155) is what Professor Anderson says: "the idea of necessity provides a binding link amidst the variety of Greek ontologies." Moreover, however much scholasticism may have recast Greek metaphysics, Dewart would insist that it does not succeed in surpassing this idea of necessity entirely (p. 208 and Dewart's recent article in *Commonweal,* Feb. 10, 1967).

In short, although Professor Anderson would agree that "as believers we are not wedded to any particular speculative tradition, Western or Eastern," yet he also believes "that 'the real distinction' is conceptually indispensable in a world of Christian theism." Likewise, although he would "concur in cultivating a Christian metaphysics" in Dewart's sense of the term, yet he seems equally determined that it be "*esse*-centered." Nor is it at all clear to me that "presence," as Dewart uses the term (p. 185), or as I use it (*Ideology and Analysis,* Part IV), or as Heidegger and Marcel use it—"is but an emphatic name for 'Being.'" (Nor can I follow the logic of the "rhetorical question": "If 'being' is an indispensable word in *many* languages, then is it not notionally essential to them *all?*")

To dehellenize is not to deny that we have not yet been able "to get along without the legacy of the Greeks," nor is it to deny that "Western man has not conceived himself to be fully human without being at least partly Greek." It is for this very reason that dehellenization is a radical proposal in that it involves a recognition of the importance of this tradition in proposing a critical reflection upon the Greek roots of the Christian conceptualization of belief and of God. Whether or not such an undertaking proves too radical and goes too far, as Professor Anderson seems to suggest, is not going to be decided merely by continuing to develop Christian theism out of Greek metaphysics. This latter, current method of integrating and developing our Greek conceptual heritage has failed to project a future of belief which is even adequate for the present. Can man surpass his cultural tradition, and specifically can Western man surpass his Greek cultural tradition? At least Anderson and Dewart would seem to agree that we cannot do so without recognizing and understanding its import and weight upon us. But to deny the success of Dewart's more radical proposal of dehellenization merely by insisting that "conceptualization is not wholly an historical process by which consciousness evolves . . . . because there *are* translations"—this is hardly, in my opinion, sufficient ground for not taking the project of dehellenization seriously.

Let us hope that *The Future of Belief* will continue to evoke the sustained dialogue, analyses and criticisms which the depth and difficulty of its proposals deserve.

III.

Neo-Thomism and the Continuity of Philosophical Experience

An Afterword

LESLIE DEWART

I

SEVERAL OF MY CRITICS have, for diverse and sometimes oppo-site reasons, reproachfully remarked upon my intense preoccupa-tion with the work of Jacques Maritain and Etienne Gilson. I confess I am somewhat surprised by this sort of reaction. I should have imagined that for a Catholic thinker to pay close attention to the doctrine of the two most influential Catholic philosophers of the first half of this century should hardly require justification —and that to pay close *critical* attention to them would have been deemed part of any philosopher's daily task. I say this be-cause, as I take up once again the topic of my relations to the thought of Gilson and Maritain, I wish to make it clear that I am not at all inclined to apologize for not having written the book that someone else, or his opponent, would have written (with undoubtedly greater success than I) had either of them held my pen in his hand. I take up this topic only because it is a matter of biographical fact that Gilson and Maritain have been among the chief philosophical influences I have undergone, and it may be that the lesson I have learned from them could be usefully recited in the hearing of others at this time. I have, of course, ended up with conclusions diametrically opposed to Gilson's and Maritain's: what they have taught me is scarcely what they would have wished to teach anyone. Nonetheless, from them I have learned certain disparate, though complementary, truths without which I would never have written as I have.

I have long and deeply esteemed Maritain's thought. It was not simply the discernment of his penetrating mind which I admired, but above all his *style* of philosophizing, which even today I take in many respects as a model of the Catholic philosophical life.[1] His taste for discovering whatever truth might be gleaned from those very philosophies which one judges, as a whole, to be mistaken, can be profitably acquired by any one, but especially perhaps by the Christian thinker. For I take it that the *catholicity* of Christian philosophy should be manifested in a greater concern for profiting from the truth than for stamping out error—on the ground, if no better could be found, that it would be a worse mistake accidentally to reject the truth than accidentally to miss it.

Under Maritain's style I would also include a quasi-congenital disposition to philosophize in dialogue with contemporary thought. Of course, it is fairly clear from much of his work—and it is definitely confirmed by *Le Paysan de la Garonne*—that most of Maritain's dialogue with the twentieth century is a monumental exercise in cross-purposes, and that his conversation with the world of modern experience is frustrated by philosophical presuppositions which, to him, are beyond all possible criticism since they are necessarily connected with Christian

1. I prescind here, of course, from the invectiveness and bitterness of *Le Paysan de la Garonne* (Paris, 1966), already foreshadowed by certain of his earliest writings, but nonetheless atypical of his best work.

belief.[2] Nevertheless, Maritain must be credited with an exemplar confidence, especially daring in the aftermath of the modernist crisis, in the value of the Christian community's dialogue with its own milieu, however deep their mutual alienation. If other Catholic thinkers in more recent times manage to communicate better with, and thus profit more from, the thought of non-Catholics and non-believers of today and of the recent past, much of the reason is to be found in Maritain's pioneering in this area during a very trying period when it was dangerous for Catholic thinkers to venture beyond the high-hedged kindergartens mapped out and established for the upbringing of Catholic philosophical thought. Maritain's insistence, for example, upon the validity of experimental science "in its own order" is the sort of thing which we can take for granted today. But we can do so only because of his work, and that of others like him; to look down upon him for his "backwardness" is to judge him anachronistically. Yet, those who so judge him, or anyone, are less unfair to him than to themselves. For those who forget that as little as a generation ago Maritain was highly suspect in certain ecclesiastical circles, and that at one time he was in great fear of having some of his propositions condemned and his works placed in the Index, may be carving out for themselves a niche in the same sort of philosophical hell into which so many have fallen—including, most regrettably, Maritain himself. Or is not the upshot of Maritain's career in the bitterness of *Le Paysan de la Garonne* a warning, a sobering lesson to us all, against attempting to philosophize from a standpoint above history and time? At any rate, though I disagree cordially with the viewpoint of Gilson and Maritain, I have none but the highest respect for their excellence, for the magnificence of their work and their obvious intellectual power. I cannot dredge up a like degree of sympathy with those who belittle their achievements—especially if they

2. This is especially evident in *Le Paysan de la Garonne,* e.g. pp. 148–149.

do so covertly [2a]—or for those who, on the contrary, identify respect with subservience, and act as if to learn from a master meant the same as to establish him upon a throne.

If I have reached, however, despite my admiration for Maritain, positions so radically divergent from his, and if I have rejected his a-historical, a-cultural conception of philosophy and his (literally) *faithful* attachment to the fundamental epistemological and metaphysical principles of St. Thomas, no small part of the reason is that from Gilson I have learned to appreciate the dialectical nature of the history of the philosophical endeavour of the human mind. Now, since the publication of *The Future of Belief* I have been told by Thomists of every kind that I do not understand the thought of St. Thomas. It would be relevant to observe that these critics, Maritainians or Maréchallians, Lonerganians or Gilsonians, transcendentalists or traditionalists, Old World or New, have yet to confront me with any evidence of my misunderstanding of St. Thomas other than the fact that my conclusions about the nature and historical role of his doctrine differ from theirs. They argue, in effect, from their own authority. However, even if they did not contradict each other on the meaning of the most elementary philosophical doctrines of St. Thomas and, indeed, on the nature of Thomism itself, I could scarcely give credence to the argument that I must be mistaken because I could not possibly be right. But I will leave this aside, for the point I wish to make at this time is not that my interpretation of St. Thomas is correct. My point is that if I have misunderstood St. Thomas, as I may well have, I must have misunderstood Gilson first.

For it was as a student of Gilson's work on the history of mediaeval philosophy that I first became aware of the cultural and historical nature of philosophical investigation. This was

2a. And least of all if insult is added. (Cf. the use of the term "woodenheaded" elsewhere in this book.)

exemplified most clearly in the emergence of St. Thomas himself, whom I learned to see in perfect continuity with the philosophical tradition behind him, and whose creativity and achievements so clearly depended upon his uninterrupted intercourse with his age. And the very idea that St. Thomas did not merely adopt Aristotle, but transformed him, (sometimes unaware, perhaps, that he had done so), bespoke to me the undesirability, if not also the impossibility, of attempting to repeat anyone's philosophy outside its original context.

Perhaps I drew the wrong lesson from such works as *The Unity of Philosophical Experience*. But when the occasion arose for me to analyze in some detail Descartes' *Meditations* and *Rules* I discovered the astonishingly simple truth that Descartes neither began a new period in the history of philosophy, nor intellectually harked back to pre-mediaeval antecedents. He seemed rather to assume all the basic presuppositions and attitudes of Scholasticism, including those of St. Thomas himself. I gradually began to realize the value, but also the incompleteness, of Gilson's work on *Le Rôle de la Pensée Médiaévale dans la Formation du Système Cartésien*. For to become aware of the many ways in which Descartes continued the historical development of philosophy after the middle ages was also to question the implicit idea, so fundamental to the neo-Thomistic *Weltanschauung,* that there was a *discontinuity* in the history of Western philosophy at the very point marked by the last word of St. Thomas and the first word of Descartes. The point merits explaining at some length.

II

For all its sophistication and its careful qualifications, the historical overview of Gilson and most neo-Thomists at bottom supposes an impossibly simple idea: that whereas all philosophy prior to St. Thomas logically led to St. Thomas, and whereas all philosophy after Descartes logically led to the inexhaustible variety of modern errors (to the intellectual excellence of which, nonetheless, left-handed compliments are very much *de rigueur*), the period between St. Thomas and Descartes was occupied exclusively by universal misunderstanding of St. Thomas. Its total achievement was to prepare the world for the errors of Descartes. The logic of this is of course impeccable: to safeguard the finality of the (admittedly partial) truth of St. Thomas's doctrine it is necessary to separate him from his Scholastic successors. Decadent Scholasticism is the indispensable scapegoat of neo-Thomism. A radical failure of the mechanism of philosophical tradition, a catastrophe in the history of ideas, is required in order to uphold the view that—with but minor, historically excusable exceptions which never affected his "principles"—a timeless truth, and nothing but the truth, had ever issued from St. Thomas's mind.

The irony is that Gilson's very understanding of the *development* of philosophy makes this interpretation of history intrinsically unlikely. If the history of philosophy is meaningful, it is difficult to believe that no one, not a single person anywhere at any time, had understood the real meaning of St. Thomas, until the truth suddenly came to Gilson between the 4th and the 5th editions of *Le Thomisme*. Now, it is not impossibly difficult to suppose that before Gilson there had existed no mind equal to the task of fully penetrating St. Thomas's own in almost 700 years. What is truly difficult to suppose, once we assume that a historical logic operates in the creation of any given philosopher's doctrine, is that the discovery of the real meaning of Thomism was itself not historically conditioned. In other words, a *historical* explanation of Gilson's own thought, of *Gilson's* interpretation of St. Thomas, is surely necessary. If no one had ever grasped St.

216

Thomas's "existentialism," why was it suddenly discovered by Gilson in 1948?

As William Barrett has pointed out, "the earlier interpretations of St. Thomas by Gilson do not mention at all a metaphysical revolution . . . that Gilson's later interpretations posit as the very core of Thomistic thought. The earlier interpretations date from years long before the popular advent of existentialism. So far as they read anything back into the text of St. Thomas from a contemporary context it is the then current controversy between realism and idealism, and St. Thomas is extolled primarily as a realist—in the midst of a then current boom of the revival of realism earlier in this century." [3] One cannot escape the initial suspicion that the real explanation of Gilson's discovery is to be found in that topsy-turvy mode of historical reasoning according to which all philosophical truth must be at least implicit in St. Thomas.

One must remember the extremes to which philosophical discipleship has been carried by neo-Thomists. Have we not all frequently heard the many variations on the same theme? If there is any truth in existentialism then St. Thomas must have been an existentialist—indeed, he was the "true" one. If any validity must, in the end, be granted to evolution, to Marxism or to psychoanalysis, graceful admissions are less likely to be forthcoming than triumphal discoveries: It *does* seem, after all, that St. Thomas can be credited with having laid down, "in a sense", the principles that made possible whatever truth these later developments contain. Should anyone be astonished if it were now proven that in St. Thomas's theory of communication the medium is the message? Rather, one can anticipate certain commentaries of John of St. Thomas on the "formal sign" which could be trotted out. I have actually heard one of Gilson's best-known pupils says—I

3. William Barrett and Henry D. Aiken, *Philosophy in the Twentieth Century* (New York, 1962), vol. II, p. 622.

think he was serious—that according to St. Thomas man does not really have a fixed and immutable nature, except in the sense that man's situation inexorably requires him to determine himself to be what he is. This was, of course, supported with a text: *anima est quoddammodo omnia.*

Evidently, if one allows the principle that all truth is implicit in St. Thomas to rule one's interpretation of history, one can with circular safety project whatever truth one learns from the present into one's philosophical past. Conversely, no error will ever be found in St. Thomas, however diligently and "openly" his works are searched. For example, since Descartes was mistaken, St. Thomas could in no way have provided any premise for his thought.

There is a curious transposition here, to the order of philosophy, of an ancient Christian belief in the catholicity of Christian truth. But it is only because the Christian believes in the essentially "revealed" character of Christain truth that he may have some warrant for judging every religious truth, wherever and whenever it may be found, to be in a real sense a manifestation of the Christian truth. Indeed, this should be better put conversely: it is not so much that the Christian revelation is the "source" of all truth, but that all truth, even that which in point of historical and cultural fact does not flow from Christianity, is justifiably "reduced" to the truth of Christianity. But "reduced" is, of course, equally misleading, for this "reduction" should not take away the possibility of a genuine development within the Christian truth, or of a real historical discontinuity between Christianity and another religious truth. It simply points to the justification of establishing *ex post facto* a connection between any religious truth and the original Christian truth, even when no such connection exists historically or culturally. For the implication here is that the Christian truth in question is "revealed." In fact, to say that it is "revealed" is to say that such a "reduction" is justified.

But, of course, this catholicity obtains, as best, in the case of revealed truth. To treat philosophical thought in the same manner would be to idolize it, to ascribe to it a divine character. And this is a procedure which the Christian believer who remembers the first commandment could not imperturbably contemplate.

My realization of all this was, of course, somewhat like an inland peasant's discovery of the Mediterranean: it was the essence of every contemporary criticism levelled at neo-Thomism as a discipline. My more original perception, however, was that Thomistic discipleship did violence to that historical understanding of philosophical development which I had first learned from *Gilson* himself. The outcome of my study of Descartes was the belief that Gilson's historical perspective was but a curious, ironic reversal of the antihistorical prejudice of so many non-Christian philosophers of recent times, who have much too easily assumed that Western philosophy began in earnest only with Descartes. Thomists now supposed, in effect, that for all practical purposes philosophical truth had unfortunately ended with St. Thomas— though the neo-Thomistic revival promised that it might be cultivated once again. Whereas the former supposed that Descartes began the age of truth, the Thomists supposed that he began the age of error—uncritically assuming that, at any rate, he began a new age, essentially discontinuous with the past at least in what pertained to error and truth. Neo-Thomism was in essence an attempt to put philosophy back on its track. The necessary basis of this idea was, of course, the supposition that at the death of St. Thomas philosophy had become derailed. And this is precisely what an unprejudiced examination of the history of philosophy shows *not* to have occurred.

It was not, however, until long after the publication of his *Elements of Christian Philosophy* that I was able to pinpoint the crucial flaw in Gilson's interpretation of the history of philosophy and, thus, to demonstrate to my own satisfaction exactly how neo-Thomistic discipleship proceeded to distort history in face of the most verifiable evidence. In that book, after quoting St. Thomas's text from *De Ente et Essentia* establishing the real distinction in created being between essence and existence, Gilson cast about through several pages looking for the basis of St. Thomas's doctrine, and finally decided that "all the arguments one can use to establish the distinction between being and essence in Thomas Aquinas's doctrine presuppose the prior recognition of the notion of the 'act of being' (*esse*)," and that "it is at least possible that the Thomistic notion of being was born at the moment when, for the first time, a metaphysician fully informed of the philosphical history of the notion happened to be, at the same time, a theologian fully conversant with [Exodus 3:14]." [4]

It appeared to me that Gilson was undoubtedly right in observing that the real distinction is not really demonstrated *a posteriori* when it is supported only by the argument that empirically given beings are *created*. For this argument really amounts to saying, "only that, in a created universe, existence must come to essences from outside and, therefore, be superadded to them." [5] In other words, this argument is *a priori:* it depends on the premise that there is a creator who is subsistent Being itself, in whom alone essence and *esse* are the same. So far I could hardly disagree. But Gilson *further* concluded that, although in the doctrine of St. Thomas "it can be demonstrated that no essence is the cause of its own existence, from which it follows that whatever has an essence, and exists, must exist in virtue of an external cause," [6] St. Thomas had given *no* demonstration of the real distinction of essence and existence *in empirically given beings as such*. In fact, said Gilson, "no one has ever been able

4. Etienne Gilson, *Elements of Christian Philosophy* (New York, 1960), pp. 130, 132.
5. *Ibid.*, p. 128.
6. *Ibid.*

to demonstrate the conclusion that, in a caused substance, existence is a distinct element, other than essence, and its act." [7] Thus, in the doctrine of St. Thomas no answer is given to the question "how do we know that empirically given beings are compounded of essence and existence?" [8]

Apart from the implication that this interpretation clearly places the whole of St. Thomas's "existentialism" in the realm of the *a priori*, I was interested in observing that Gilson's elucubrations were quite unnecessary. For it was not in principle impossible that St. Thomas, given the primitive stage of development of exegesis at the time, might have indeed derived his metaphysical inspiration from Exodus 3:14. It was beyond question, of course, that St. Thomas did interpret this text in accordance with his metaphysics of essence and existence; and it did seem most likely that in point of fact his inspiration depended, in any event, upon that basic attitude of the Christian faith towards empirical reality which regards it as totally contingent, a gratuitous creation of God, God's gift of being to itself. But the curious thing was that in the very text that Gilson had quoted, just before puzzling out the matter to an inconclusive finish, St. Thomas himself *had* explicitly and unequivocally given the *empirical* basis on which he grounded the real distinction in empirically given beings *as such*. I have quoted it in *The Future of Belief:* "Now, every essence or quiddity can be understood without anything being known of its existing. I can know what a man or a phoenix is and still be ignorant whether it exists in reality. *From this it is clear that* the act of existing is other than essence or quiddity, unless, perhaps, there is a being whose quiddity is its very act of existing. And there can be only one such being, the First Being." [9]

7. *Ibid.*
8. *Ibid.*, p. 127.
9. St. Thomas Aquinas, *De Ente et Essentia,* IV; Maurer translation, p. 46.

I should apologize for belaboring the obvious, were it not that in this context the obvious seems to have escaped both Gilson and Maritain. The text says: "from this it is clear that." This sentence seems to me unequivocally to refer to an antecedent premise, "this," and to a consequent conclusion, "that." The conclusion is that "the act of existing is other than essence or quiddity" (though the possibility is left open that there might be a whose quiddity is its very act of existing"). Does this refer *formally* to empirically given being? Or is it applicable to empirically given being only insofar as it is created? The conclusion by itself does not state which. But its meaning should be clear from the context, that is, from its relation to the premise. Now, what is the premise on which this conclusion is based? The text states it: it is an empirical observation, namely, that "every essence or quiddity can be understood without anything being known of its existing." Is this not an observation about empirically given being as such? If any doubt should remain the example which St. Thomas adds should dispel it. For the text does *not* say: "a man or a phoenix can be conceived by God and yet not be brought into existence." It says: "*I can know* what a man or a phoenix is and still *be ignorant* whether it exists in reality." Of course, this may well have been more than St. Thomas had bargained for. Note that an observation about empirically given being as such concerns *being,* to be sure, but being insofar as it is *given* in experience: it has to do with what "I can know" and with what I can "be ignorant" of. It is, thus, an observation about experience itself—not, of course, about the dynamics or the functioning of the mind, but about its "contents."

From this I conclude, contrary to Gilson, that St. Thomas *did* provide an empirical basis for the real distinction between essence and existence in empirically given being as such. The basis of the real distinction between essence and existence in creatures—or, to put it formally, in *empirically given being*—is an empirical observation, namely, that which I have quoted above. And this empirical observation implies an empirical reflection upon that which is given in experience as such. Though St. Thomas was probably not aware of what he was in fact doing, the fact is that he based the real distinction upon a reflexive analysis of experience itself.

But I could understand the reluctance—surely unconscious—of Gilson to read the text of St. Thomas at face value, and his reduction of St. Thomas's argument to Avicenna's,[10] ignoring altogether the evidence that lay before his eyes. For to take this text at face value is to grant that the *problematic* existence of objects of knowledge as such was implicit in this, the most basic metaphysical doctrine of St. Thomas. In other words, if St. Thomas meant exactly what he said in this text (that is, if the *empirical* reason why essence and existence are distinct *in empirically given being* is the *empirical* fact that in such being essence can be known without actual existence being *ipso facto* known), then the philosophy of Descartes would sooner or later logically arise on the very basis provided by St. Thomas, namely, *a reflexive analysis of empirical knowledge itself*. But if this was true, the bubble syllogism on which neo-Thomism had been established was burst.

III

Let us, therefore, briefly consider how the philosophy of Descartes arose on the basis provided by St. Thomas and, thus, in continuity with it.

The key discontinuity between St. Thomas and Descartes is supposedly found, of course, in their epistemologies. According

10. Gilson, p. 127.

to neo-Thomists this discontinuity is very easily shown. In St. Thomas's theory of knowledge, that which is known, *id quod,* is not in the first instance the concept, *id quo,* but the very *thing* which exists outside the mind and which faces the mind. The concept is not *id quod,* but *id quo.* Descartes' difficulty—how to transcend the dichotomy of concept and thing—does not arise in Thomism, for knowing is precisely the transcending of this dichotomy. For it is a *fact* that we know: this is the fact from which a philosophical investigation of knowledge begins. After Descartes philosophy wrestled with a pseudo-problem, and Thomistic realism remains, therefore, sufficient unto this day.

The trouble with this argument is that it is largely true—but that nevertheless the conclusion does not follow. For there are additional considerations which change its complexion. The first of these is the distinction between a *theory* of knowledge and a *concept* of knowledge. The most basic continuity of Western philosophy depends not so much on the logical connection among the varieties of *theories* of knowledge, but upon the invariance, until recent times, of the *concept* of knowledge. For all their differences in theory of knowledge, Descartes and St. Thomas shared a common *concept* of knowledge: to know is to transcend the duality of two things, knower and known. Descartes never doubted this—any more than St. Thomas did. This is why Descartes, no more than St. Thomas ever had any *real doubt* that the known is, *in point of fact,* an extramental existent. Indeed, the whole effort of Descartes' epistemology is to demonstrate philosophically what he assumed to be true in any event. But note the implication: though Descartes, so far as his writings indicate, never entertained a real doubt concerning the extramental existence of objects of knowledge, nevertheless this extramental existence was for him *philosophically problematic.* To solve this problem, he thought, it was necessary for philosophy to entertain not a *real,* but a *methodic,* doubt.

224

Now, given Descartes' concept of knowledge, which he held in common with St. Thomas, why did Descartes, *unlike St. Thomas,* think that the existence of the extramental known was problematic, and that the solution required a methodic doubt of that existence? Thomists have not resolutely faced this question. The answer leads directly to the conclusion already suggested above.

Like every other philosopher between Parmenides and Hegel, St. Thomas conceived knowledge as the act whereby the mind grasps something beyond itself (in the case of direct knowledge) or, at any rate, (whether in direct or reflexive knowledge), something beyond the mind's act itself. The process by which the ordinary fact of knowledge is theoretically explained by St. Thomas is irrelevant to present purposes. What matters is that St. Thomas also developed the corresponding metaphysics noted above, in which the contingency of created being (a concept which expresses a matter of Christian faith) was philosophically explained by the real distinction between essence and existence. But, empiricist that he was, St. Thomas did not assert this distinction *a priori:* he grounded it, as we have seen, on the empirical observation that "every essence or quiddity can be understood without anything being known of its existing."

St. Thomas did not attempt to incorporate this view into his theory of knowledge: it is a loose end, asserted but once, and in an early work. Nonetheless this observation provided him with the premise on which to base the identity of essence and existence in God—which thereafter became the effective principle from which to argue that if God exists and is self-subsistent Being, then essence and existence are distinct in created being. After St. Thomas, the real distinction became a philosophical commonplace—though the empirical foundation on which it rested was not always kept in mind. But sooner or later someone was bound to draw the inevitable consequences from the fact that the contingency of creatures (precisely as conceptualized in terms of the real distinction between essence and existence) was grounded upon a characteristic of creatures insofar as they were *objects of knowledge*. Sooner or later someone was bound to realize that if the contingency of those creatures which are the objects of our empirical knowledge becomes evident to us only by virtue of their properties as objects of empirical knowledge, then it follows that we can never assert that any being actually exists, simply on the ground that we know it. (Indeed, idealism eventually arose as a hypothesis that would render this assertion possible despite the real distinction between essence and existence, which after St. Thomas and until our own century continued to be tacitly assumed by everyone.)

In other words, if by knowledge we attain to an extramental reality which does not necessarily exist and which indeed (since this is the basis of the foregoing assertion) cannot, simply because it is known, be necessarily known to exist, then the existence of every known extramental being is philosophically problematic. But note: it is *only philosophically* problematic. Why? Because according to the common concept of knowledge which still underlies this reasoning (namely, the concept of knowledge as the mind's intentional intussusception of an extramental reality), no *real* doubt about that existence can be entertained.

This dual affirmation was, of course, essential to Descartes' problem: how to establish *philosophically* the real existence of objects of knowledge about whose real existence common sense has no *real* doubt—for indeed their real existence is *presupposed* by the common-sense concept of knowledge. But whereas Descartes and modern philosophy after him so emphasized the *philosophically problematic* character of objects of knowledge that ultimately then were impotent to establish the rationality of affirming the actual existence of extramental objects about whose actual existence *no real doubt* could be entertained, Maritain and Gilson, together with most modern realists, have emphasized the epistemological value of the assertion that *no real doubt* about the existence of extramental objects of knowledge can be reasonably entertained. But since the latter emphasis entailed the denial of the *philosophically problematic* character of objects of knowledge, and since Maritain and Gilson have been unable to suppose that St. Thomas's thought could be inadequate in any basic respect, they have logically attributed the emergence of the Cartesian problem to the total and unrelieved misunderstanding of St. Thomas by every later generation culminating in Descartes. This is, as I have remarked, perfectly self-consistent: the essential infallibility of St. Thomas's philosophy *can* be upheld—if only one is willing to read the history of philosophy backwards (or else not at all).

But if we look at the matter straightforwardly, the continuity of philosophical experience after St. Thomas (and not only after Descartes) is not difficult to discern. In fact, it is a tribute to Descartes' ingenuity that the very terms of the problem he inherited suggested to him the direction in which the solution lay.

As posed above, the problem could be solved only through a *methodic doubt* of the existence of the extramental being which is the object of knowledge. For, if we assume that knowledge does in fact unite to the mind an extramental reality whose existence is philosophically problematic, then the nub of the problem is this: the same empirical observations which, on the one hand, are enshrined in the common-sense concept of knowledge, also imply, on the other, that there can be no empirical difference between an act of knowledge of a quiddity which actually exists extramentally, and an act of knowledge of a quiddity which does not. Therefore, although the existence of the extramental known cannot be really doubted and should be, surely, demonstrable (unless we admit the alternative of skepticism), this real existence cannot be philosophically demonstrated except perhaps on the methodological hypothesis that knowledge would be possible even in the absence of an extramental existent. For it follows from St. Thomas's grounding of the real distinction *upon a reflexive analysis of knowledge,* that there could be no empirically detectable difference between knowing *id quod,* (that which is known), and knowing *id quo,* (that by which we know that which exists extramentally). Therefore, the demonstration must proceed *as if* what were known were *only id quo,* that is, *as if* it were only an idea within the mind. The first *Meditation* of Descartes is devoted to nothing but this very point.

The remainder of Descartes' train of thought is history. But we cannot divorce what happened after Descartes from what happened before him. Descartes began—though he hardly realized it himself—the long process of bringing to the surface the inadequacy and insufficiency of the traditional, hellenic *concept* of knowledge: he did this when he attempted to integrate contradictory elements in St. Thomas's thought. But this means: philosophy neither began with Descartes nor ended with St. Thomas. So far as I know it began, in our tradition, with the pre-Socratics—and it has not ended yet. Nor did its history suddenly become discontinuous at a certain point in time. The continuity of philosophical experience from St. Thomas to Descartes is not only deducible *a priori,* from our knowledge of the historical manner in which philosophy appears to develop at all times. It is also demonstrable *a posteriori,* from a consideration of the doctrines themselves. And philosophy has not merely a chronology, it is not merely a logical succession of events. Philosophy is historical in its very nature, for historicity is of the very nature of human thought.

The enormity of the challenge hurled at Catholic philosophy by the fairly recently acquired human consciousness of the historicity of all thought may be easily imagined, even on the basis of the foregoing considerations alone. Many Catholic thinkers will find this challenge overwhelming, and may pretend that if they do not take it up the only reason is that the problem is specious, that the challenge does not really exist. Or if they admit it exists, they will deal with it as with a threat, supposing that the problem arises not from the normal, natural, creative development of thought, but from man's sinful perversion of his intellect.

Whether it will be this sort of viewpoint or its opposite that will in fact finally define the future orientation of Catholic philosophy is a question to which we shall not have an answer prior to the event. For neither viewpoint is destined to prevail. The very historicity of thought means that philosophical development is not the unfolding of logical necessities potentially contained in the historical premises of thought. If, like all thought, philosophy develops creatively, the logic of the history of philosophy does not mean that its issue is fated in advance. Thus, whichever course the collective Catholic intellect decides upon, it will be the outcome of its creativity and its freedom. Whatever it brings about, it shall be responsible for—whether it brings it about responsibly or not.

Notes on Contributors

BARNABAS AHERN is Professor of Sacred Scripture at St. Meinrad Seminary, and the author of *New Horizons*.

JAMES F. ANDERSON is Professor of Philosophy at Villanova University, and the author of *The Bond of Being*.

GREGORY BAUM is Director of the Centre of Ecumenical Studies at St. Michael's College, Toronto, and editor of *The Ecumenist*.

HARVEY COX is Professor of Theology at Harvard Divinity School, and the author of *The Secular City*.

EUGENE FONTINELL is Professor of Philosophy at Queens College.

ARTHUR GIBSON is Professor of Theology at St. Michael's College, Toronto.

R. C. HINNERS is Professor of Philosophy at Loyola College, Montreal, and the author of *Ideology and Analysis*.

H. DE LAVALETTE is Professor of Theology at the Institut Catholique, Paris, and a contributing editor of *Etudes*.

BERNARD J. F. LONERGAN is Professor of Theology at the Gregorianum University, Rome, and the author of *Insight*.

JOSEPH OWENS is Professor of Philosophy at the Pontifical Institute for Medieval Studies, Toronto, and the author of *St. Thomas and the Future of Metaphysics*.

JAROSLAV PELIKAN is Titus Street Professor of Ecclesiastical History at Yale Divinity School, and the author of *The Riddle of Roman Catholicism*.

ILLTYD TRETHOWAN is a monk of Downside Abbey, and former editor of the *Downside Review*.

JOHN W. M. VERHAAR is Professor of Philosophy at the Ateneo de Manila.

BRIAN WICKER is on the Faculty of Humanities at the University of Birmingham, and the author of *Culture and Liturgy*.

FREDERICK WILHELMSEN is Professor of Philosophy at the University of Dallas, a member of the editorial staff of *Triumph*, and the author of *Metaphysics of Love*.